Born of the Water
Born of the Spirit

Dr. Ernest S. Martin

Copyright 2024 by Dr. Ernest S. Martin

ISBN: 978-1-961225-73-2 (Paperback)
ISBN: 978-1-961225-74-9 (Hardback)
ISBN: 978-1-961225-75-6 (Ebook)

All rights reserved. This book or any portion thereof may not be reproduced or used in any manner whatsoever without the express written permission of the publisher except for the use of brief quotation in a book review.

Printed in the United States of America

CONTENTS

Acknowledgement vi
Foreword vii
Introduction ix

Part 1 1
Conception: Receiving God's Promise 3
    Fertilize or Perish 6
    Hormones and the Holy Spirit 7
    Many Are Called 10
    From Darkness into Light 13
    The Witnesses of Christ 14
    Two Ways to Heaven 16
    The Path to Conception 18
    Conception and Conversion 22
    The Miracle of Salvation 25
    Spiritual "Contraception" 26

Part 2 30
Gestation: Growing Up into Christ 31
    Sealed by the Spirit 32
    Abiding in Christ 34
    Dividing God's Word 35
    God's Blueprint for Development 36
    Building on the Rock 38
    Experience vs. God's Word 41
    God's Structural Test 43
    Entering into God's Rest 45

God's Rest in Action 48
The Natural Walk. 51
An Effective Witness. 57
No Respecter of Persons. 61
The Body of Christ 66

Part 3. 72
The Live Birth: God's Promise Fulfilled. 73
In His Image. 75
Understanding Salvation 78
Sealed in Christ 80
Faith and Works. 85
The Enemy of Faith 87
Counting the Cost 91
Marriage Made in Heaven 98
At Home with God. 100

Conclusion 103
A Word from the Author 103
About the Author. 108

The Salvation Process from Conception to Birth

Acknowledgement

Heartfelt gratitude to Bryan Wayne Stuckey and his wife Maryjane who spent countless hours transcribing the tapes from the sermons I preached on the relationship of physical birth to spiritual birth. They also designed most of the artwork for this book. I am extremely grateful for their diligent and excellent literary, editing, and artistic skills that made this book, *Born of the Water Born of the Spirit*, a reality.

Foreword

Let another man praise thee, and not thine own mouth.
—Proverbs 27:2

For a period of time, I think that I perceived Dr. Martin as a person born with an additional *superhuman* gene that—for some unexplained, providential reason—had been withheld from the rest of us struggling to make spiritual sense of our lives. How else could a man remain diligent, humble, and above reproach, all the while juggling a stable marriage, four active boys, a deep relationship with God, a successful full-time veterinary practice, and the pastorate of a small nondenominational church in the heart of Dallas, Texas?

I would learn—to my surprise—that this seeming paragon had, in fact, sprung from the same pitiable protoplasm as my own self, with all of the inherent flaws and weaknesses of mankind. No, there was no great moral failure required on his part for me to come to this revelation, just a gradual recognition that this man quite reasonably took no credit for the supernatural moving of God in his life— a man who spoke far more highly of his talented and faithful wife than he would ever think of speaking of himself. I recall one Wednesday evening when he opened a service so totally exhausted from a busy day at his hospital that he closed his eyes and began—to the loving and familial chuckles of the small group in attendance—to bless the "food." But God had indeed prepared the table, and this reluctant prophet proceeded to bring another powerfully anointed message.

The secret? It became evident that this country boy from North Dakota—who frequently performed pastoral counselling in between surgeries on dogs and cats—had stumbled upon a disturbingly primitive spiritual formula. He had learned to simply *trust God*. Reserved in public but bold in pulpit, he would often relate the words God had spoken to his spirit at the beginning of his ministry: "I want you to forget every doctrine and tradition of men that you have ever been taught, and I will teach you Myself out of My Word." The result has been an unselfish, Word-centered life and ministry both in and outside of the Church with consequences that have been eminently practical and life-changing for many of us.

Bryan Wayne Stuckey

Introduction

Ironically, the most misunderstood doctrine in the Bible, and consequently in the Church today, is that of *salvation*. Terms like "saved" and "born again" are invoked by saints and sinners alike, but behind the vernacular of Christianity, there is an astounding amount of confusion associated with this very basic scriptural tenet.

It was no accident that Jesus used the phrase "Ye must be born again" in His discourse with Nicodemus in John's Gospel, nor was it by chance that God spoke the words "Let Us create man in Our image" in Genesis 1. We should not be surprised to find that the physical is often a reflection of what actually exists and evolves in the spiritual realm. Nowhere is this more beautifully illustrated than in the human body as we examine the process of sexual reproduction. We will see, using the Word of God and a general outline of simplified anatomy and physiology, that there is an amazing—but not coincidental—parallel between the conception, gestation, and delivery of a baby—i.e., the "first" birth, and the salvation of a human soul and the "second" birth. We must be born *once* in the flesh in order to have life. We must be born *again* in the Spirit in order to have *eternal life*.

An extensive knowledge of biology is by no means a prerequisite for understanding this book; the concepts presented here are simple and straightforward. Quotations of scripture are taken from the Authorized King James Version of the Bible unless otherwise indicated; notation may be added, or punctuation and spelling modified, for the purpose of emphasis or clarification.

It is only as we seek God that the reality of His Word can be made alive in our hearts with the help of the Holy Spirit. I prayerfully trust that you will lay aside preconception and tradition as you proceed in this study, and that this book will contribute in some way to your better understanding of this most fundamental of all biblical doctrines.

Part I

Conception: Receiving God's Promise

The human body with its amazing integration of form and function remains an object of wonderment even in our sophisticated computer age. One cannot observe Olympic sports competition, for example, without some sense of awe at the design and capacity of the human machine. Science remains largely ignorant of the intricacies of the chemical computer we know as the human brain which has given birth to the spectacular technological achievements of the past century. In the context of God's Word, we find that the significance of the human body with its various specialized structures, senses and internal processes greatly transcends the one-dimensional description of textbook biology. In fact, it becomes evident that man is a distinctively *triune* entity of not only physical and mental proportion, but he must be correctly perceived as a *spiritual* being as well.

Most people who are taking the time to read this book would probably agree with me that there is an observed *order* in the natural world and throughout the universe itself that can hardly be relegated to status of mere cosmic "accident." Many scientists find it remarkable that only minor deviation from its prescribed orbit around the sun could have rendered our planet totally inhospitable to the development of life as we know it. The evidence of intelligent *design* in nature is ubiquitous; in living creatures, there are countless determinations of form, structure, color, function, and behavior that cannot entirely be explained in terms of either proven or posited mechanisms of evolutionary process. Forces of gravity and many other laws of physics—which often defy any kind of exhaustive explanation by science—maintain and regulate an enormously complex universe that would otherwise degenerate instantly into the kind of formlessness and void we find described in the first chapter of Genesis.

After looking at it closely, I came to recognize that even the prosaic biblical narrative of creation suggests the implementation of a divine, systematic *plan*. Using an indeterminate increment of celestial time referred to as a "day," this simple account describes a purposeful sequence of events in which the *first* day established the groundwork for the *fourth* day, the *second* day for the *fifth*, and the *third* day for the *sixth* (figure 1).

Day	Events	Events	Day
1	Creation of light	Creation of *instruments* of light: sun, moon, stars	4
2	Separation of water and sky	Creation of water life and flying birds	5
3	Creation of dry land and vegetation	Creation of man and animals	6

Figure 1.

Throughout the scriptures, it is manifestly clear that the God of all creation is a God of order and purpose; this applies to His activity in the spiritual world as well as in the physical. The popular notion of a parallel universe is not a new concept. In the context of spiritual authority, Jesus made the statement, "And I will give unto thee the keys of the kingdom of Heaven: and whatsoever thou shalt bind on *earth* shall be bound in *Heaven*: and whatsoever thou shalt loose on earth shall be loosed in Heaven" (Matthew 16:19). There are many things described in the Bible whose symbolic and concise dimensions, parameters and specifications were supplied by God Himself. These include the Jewish tabernacle, the ark of the covenant, the temple, and the city of Jerusalem, which are all described as "types" or "shadows"; reflections of a spiritual *reality* that is ultimately far more abiding and permanent than its physical counterpart.

In the course of their private and candid discussion of spiritual reality in John's Gospel, Jesus shocked Nicodemus by presenting a rather strange precondition for eternal life or "salvation"—a candidate must first be "reborn." In essence, what Jesus was really trying to get Nicodemus to understand was that it is not enough for the *flesh* to be born; the *spirit* must also be made alive.

When God said, "Let Us make man in Our image" (Genesis 1:26), He not only distinguished mankind from other forms of life, but He literally designed our physical image in such a way that it corresponds directly to its spiritual complement. As we look at the human body, specifically, the reproductive system of the woman, I think you will begin to better understand the process of salvation. Just as the physical miracle of bringing a new baby into the world requires conception, gestation and delivery, so the spiritual miracle of being "born again" has a beginning, a middle and an end.

Jesus and the apostle Paul both addressed the dual nature of this salvation experience:

> Jesus answered, "Verily, verily, I say unto thee, except a man be born of water and of the spirit, he cannot enter into the kingdom of God. That which is born of the flesh is flesh; and that which is born of the Spirit is spirit. Marvel not that I said unto thee, 'ye must be born again.'" (John 3:5–7)

> And as we have borne the image of the earthy, we shall also bear the image of the heavenly. (1 Corinthians 15:49)

It is evident that Jesus's reference to the "water" birth was to the physical birth. Indeed, as we can observe, the human fetus is literally immersed in water, or *amniotic fluid* within a protective sac until the time of delivery. The physical birth alone is insufficient, however, to enable anyone to enter the kingdom of God. Jesus lays out a very definite precondition for eternal life: a person must experience a *new birth*. What does this *second* birth involve?

Fertilize or Perish

When a baby girl is born, her ovarian *follicles* (figure 2) contain—in theory— all of the immature *egg* cells, or *oocytes*, that she will ever have. Of an estimated two million or so present at birth, only a few hundred oocytes (figure 3) will ultimately develop and be ovulated during the reproductive life of the woman. Of these, only the ones that are fertilized, if any, ever have any possibility of continued existence beyond the monthly menstrual cycle. If an oocyte is not fertilized, it will perish. The oocyte is a complete, living cell, but it has only twenty-three chromosomes. It must be fertilized by a sperm cell containing an equal number of chromosomes in order to form the genesis of a viable human being.

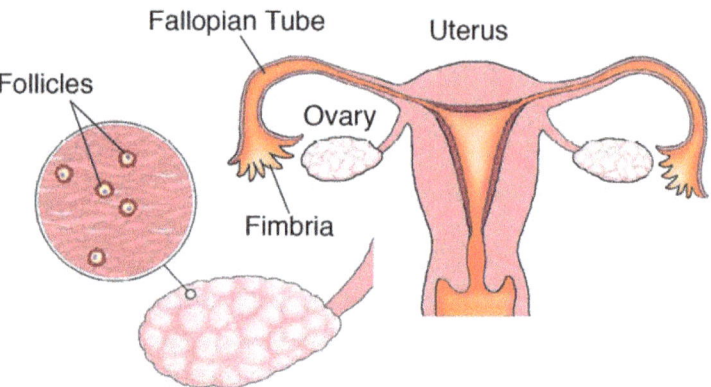

Figure 2. Ovary and Follicles

In the same way, a person who is physically born into the world is *alive*, but his or her *spirit* does not yet have life. The scripture indicates that if the Word of God does not penetrate and vitalize that spirit, that person—like the unfertilized oocyte—will *perish*. Our current understanding of physics tells us that the total amount of mass is never destroyed; it merely changes form.

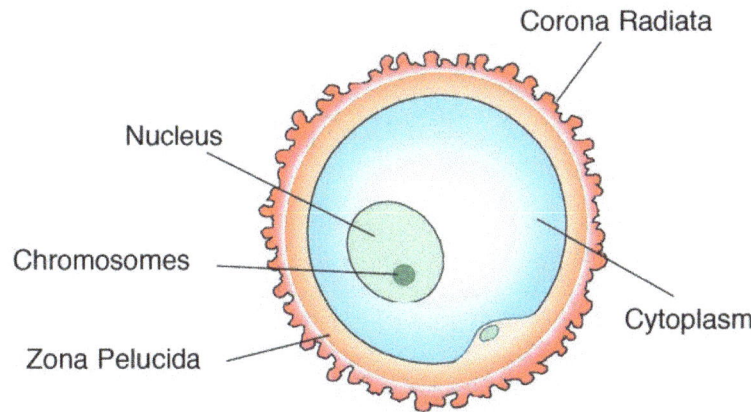

Figure 3. Oocyte

Energy within a contained system does not change, and—although it can be converted into matter and back again—it cannot be created or destroyed. Similarly, an oocyte that is not fertilized will cease to have life, but its molecular components will continue to exist in some degenerated state. At death, a person who has rejected the claims of God's Word will spend eternity in a different form, separated from God, but will be quite aware of his or her spiritual condition.

When the oocyte is fertilized by the sperm, a new *life* is created; the resulting *conceptus* is now genetically complete and has all of the potential to grow into a full-term baby. In the case of conception, "one plus one equals one." The same thing happens when you or I, on the basis of *faith*, become a *new creation* in Christ. We have been made spiritually complete and are now immature, but "whole" individuals. Our spirits have suddenly been made alive! We now have the potential to grow up into the "measure of the stature of the fullness of Christ" (Ephesians 4:13).

Hormones and the Holy Spirit.

For the purpose of our discussion, if the unfertilized oocyte represents the person without Christ, then the ovary is a diminutive picture of the world that contains that "lost" person. In and of itself, the egg cell is totally helpless. A *primary* oocyte cannot one day "decide" to ovulate, burst out of its ovarian follicle and proceed to be fertilized. Neither can a person spontaneously conjure up the faith to believe

God's Word, forsake their sinful, worldly nature and be born again on their own initiative. Certain preconditions apply in both cases.

The development of an ovarian follicle and the subsequent ovulation event are totally dependent upon the action of the hormones known as FSH (*follicle- stimulating hormone*) and LH (*luteinizing hormone*). These *gonadotropic* hormones are released into the bloodstream by the pituitary gland, which is in turn controlled by the hypothalamus in the brain. During the monthly process known as the *ovarian cycle*, several of the primary follicles containing the oocytes are stimulated by these hormones, primarily by FSH (Figure 4). Of these, generally only one will develop to maturity and rupture, resulting in the expulsion of an oocyte from the ovary. The remaining follicles within this group begin to degenerate and will never again be stimulated by hormonal activity. Consequently, the oocytes they contain perish in the ovary and will never have another opportunity to be fertilized.

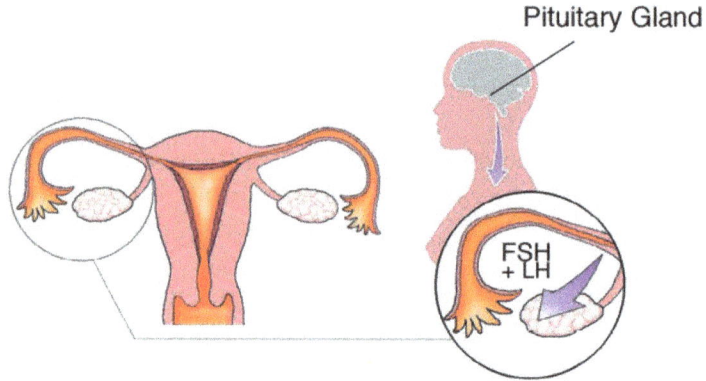

Figure 4. Follicle Stimulation

In John 15:16, Jesus makes the statement, "Ye have not chosen *Me*, but I have chosen *you*." In John 6:44 He says, "No man can come to Me, except the Father which hath sent Me *draw him*." With regard to salvation, it is apparent that God, through the Holy Spirit, must initiate the process. Just as the hypothalamus in the brain directs the release of hormones which stimulate the ovarian follicles, so Jesus Christ—the "Head" of the "Body of Christ"—directs the Holy Spirit to begin to draw a person toward God. At this point, it is not difficult to see that the function of hormones in *conception* parallels the role of the Holy Spirit in the *salvation* of a human soul! We will see that hormones continue to play a critical role not only in conception but in the maintenance of pregnancy as well.

The scripture says that "faith cometh by hearing, and hearing by the Word of God" (Romans 10:17). When we have been drawn by the Holy Spirit and are prepared to seek God, something else must be in place before we can "step out" of the world. *Faith* must be present. Faith is a *gift* from God. Romans 12:3 says that every person has been given a certain *measure* of faith. We must then act upon that faith by choosing to seek God. If we do not, that faith will "die" (James 2:17).

The action of FSH and LH upon the ovarian follicle cause it to develop to the point of ovulation (figure 5). The maturing follicle expands to many times its original size, causing a bulge on the surface of the ovary. Ovulation is no simple matter, however. The ovary and its follicles are virtually imprisoned by a layer of *collagen* fibers, a protein material known to have a tensile strength exceeding that of steel!

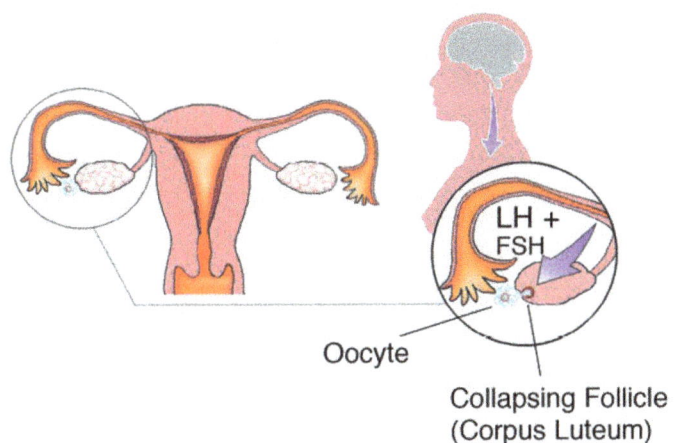

Figure 5. Ovulation

How does the helpless oocyte make its exit from this "steel prison"? Inflamed ovarian tissues, responding to heightened LH stimulation, begin to secrete the enzyme *collagenase*, which in turn begins to break down the layer of collagen. Finally, the weakened surface of the ovary ruptures like a balloon; the *secondary* oocyte and surrounding follicular fluid are expelled under pressure from the follicle into the abdominal cavity.

It is quite interesting to note that in the process of being expelled from the ovary, the developing oocyte is attended by its water bath (the clear follicular fluid) and also by a slight hemorrhage. The imagery of *water* and *blood* is repeated later with the presence of both water (clear amniotic fluid) and blood in the actual birth process. Though not fully within the scope of our study, the water/blood relationship is highly symbolic in scripture and can be clearly linked not only to the crucifixion of Christ but to some important biblical doctrines as well, including baptism and sanctification.

> This is He that came by water and blood, even Jesus Christ; not by water only, but by water and blood. And it is the Spirit that beareth witness, because the Spirit is truth. (1 John 5:6–7)

> Let us draw near with a true heart in full assurance of faith, having our hearts sprinkled [with blood] from an evil conscience and our bodies washed with pure water. (Hebrews 10:22)

It is often assumed that the oocyte is ovulated directly into the *fallopian tube*. In fact, this is not the case. Again, we find the human egg cell at the "mercy" of processes beyond its control. Quite symbolically, it is actually drawn into the fallopian tube by the gentle beckoning movements of finger-like *fimbriae* located at the end of the tube. *Ectopic* pregnancies outside of the uterine cavity itself can occur at various locations, including—in very unusual cases—the abdominal cavity. A number of complications can occur in the reproductive process, but for the present, we will focus on the normal, ideal course of pregnancy as it applies to salvation.

Many Are Called

The most sobering parallel between the physical and the spiritual thus far is the fact that out of the vast numbers of oocytes present in the ovary at birth, only a fraction will ever begin to move toward ovulation. Of these, again, only a small percentage will actually be expelled from the ovary and have any "hope" of fertilization. We find in scripture that—like the relatively small numbers of egg cells that may ultimately be "saved" out of the ovary—relatively few people will ever experience a successful entrance into the kingdom of God. Jesus said, "For *many* are called, but *few* are chosen" (Matthew 22:14). The issue is addressed in the following passage:

> Then said one unto Him, "Lord, are there few that be saved?" And He said unto them, "Strive to enter in at the [narrow] gate: for many, I say to you, will seek to enter in, and shall not be able. When once the master of the house is risen up, and hath shut to the door, and ye begin to stand without, and to knock at the door, saying, 'Lord, Lord, open unto us'; and He shall answer and say unto you, 'I know you not whence ye are': then shall ye begin to say, 'We have eaten and drunk in Thy Presence, and Thou hast taught in our streets.' But He shall say, 'I tell you, I know not whence ye are; depart from Me, all ye workers of iniquity.'" (Luke 13:23–27)

Clearly, of all the billions of people who are ever born into the world, only a small remnant—in proportional terms—are going to inherit eternal life. Again, Jesus alludes to this fact:

> Enter ye in at the [narrow] gate: for wide is the gate, and broad is the way, that leadeth to destruction, and many there be which go in thereat: because [narrow] is the gate, and [narrow] is the way, which leadeth unto life, and few there be that find it. (Matthew 7:13–14)

People frequently ask the question, "If God is a *loving* God, why would He send anyone to *hell*?" The truth is God is "not willing that any should perish" (2 Peter 3:9). The scripture also says that God has "no pleasure in the death of the wicked" (Ezekiel 33:11). God's nature is such that He would much prefer that all men repent and be "saved." Saved from *what*? The scripture answers this question quite clearly. We are saved from *perishing* at the revelation of God's judgment upon sin when—drawn supernaturally by the Holy Spirit—we believe His

Word, turn from our sins, and call upon His name in unconditional surrender to His authority in our lives.

But God commendeth His love toward us, in that, while we were yet sinners, Christ died for us. Much more then, being now justified by His blood, we shall be saved from wrath through Him. (Romans 5:8–9)

For God so loved the world, that He gave His only begotten Son, that whosoever believeth in Him should not perish, but have everlasting life. (John 3:16)

We must come to the understanding that God does not "send" anyone to hell.

We send ourselves there. I am often reminded of an allegorical story based on an actual event about a young death row inmate. The day before his execution, an older man in a dark suit came and stood by the man's cell door as if he had something to say. The inmate cursed the "preacher" and told him to leave. The visitor stood there for a moment longer and again the condemned man, cursed him, and told him to get out. At that point, the stranger turned and slowly walked away. The next day, as the guard was strapping him into the electric chair, the young man was asked by his attendant, "What did you say to that man last night?" He answered, "I told that preacher where he could get off." The guard responded, "That wasn't a preacher, that was the governor of our state. In his vest pocket, he had for you a full pardon." The doomed prisoner, broken, replied, "Tell the people of my state something for me. I didn't die because of the murder I committed but because of the pardon I refused." People do not perish because of the acts of sin they commit but, more accurately, because of the *pardon* they refuse!

For God so loved the world, that He gave His only begotten Son, that whosoever believeth in Him should not perish, but have everlasting life. For God sent not His Son into the world to condemn the world; but that the world through Him might be saved. He that believeth on Him is not condemned: but he that believeth not is condemned already, because he hath not believed in the name of the only begotten Son of God. (John 3:16–18)

In other words, it is the rejection of Jesus Christ as *Lord* and *Savior* that incurs a self-inflicted death sentence and eternal separation from God's presence. Unlike the helpless oocyte, we have been given a mind and a will. We have the ability to either choose or reject truth. Rejecting the claims of God's Word is not a sin of commission; it is a sin of omission. It is refusing Christ his rightful place in our lives. This is what "sends" a person to hell. Before we return to the topic of conception, we are going to see that God makes every effort to draw a person to Himself. The question is this: Will we respond by seeking Him?

But if from thence thou shalt seek the Lord thy God, thou shalt find Him, if thou seek Him with all thy heart and with all thy soul. (Deuteronomy 4:29)

Then shall ye call upon Me, and ye shall go and pray unto Me, and I will hearken unto you. And ye shall seek Me, and find Me when ye shall search for Me with all your heart. (Jeremiah 29:12–13)

From Darkness into Light

Perhaps the best description of the state of the unsaved person is found in Genesis 1:2, "And the earth was without form, and void; and darkness was on the face of the deep." A person outside of Christ is "void" and "without form" because there is no apparent purpose to his life. He is also in spiritual darkness, but is not aware of it. Before you are drawn to Christ, you cannot recognize that you are in this condition. Why? Because you are receiving light from the "god" of this world; Satan can even be manifested as an "angel of light" (2 Corinthians 11:14).

If you were to turn off the tungsten or fluorescent lights in a room and turn on ultraviolet, or "black" lights instead, you would be able to see and go about your activities. However, if you turned the normal lighting back on, the ultraviolet light would "disappear." The scripture tells us that Jesus Christ is the true light that God has sent into the world, but that those who are in darkness cannot comprehend this light.

In the beginning was the Word, and the Word was with God, and the Word was God. The same was in the beginning with God. All things were made by Him; and without Him was not anything made that was made. In Him was life; and the life was the light of men and the light shineth in darkness; and the darkness comprehended it not. There was a man sent from God, whose name was John. The same came for a witness, to bear witness of the light, that all men through him might believe. He was not that light, but was sent to bear witness of that light. That was the true light, which lighteth every man that cometh into the world. He was in the world, and the world was made by Him, and the world knew him not. (John 1:1–10)

Then spake Jesus again unto them, saying, "I am the light of the world: he that followeth Me shall not walk in darkness, but shall have the light of life." (John 8:12)

If you have received Christ, before you accepted Him you were "void," "without form," and in spiritual "darkness." You were just like that oocyte, hopelessly trapped with no purpose or future, as long as it remains in the ovary. Then something happened! "And the Spirit of God moved upon the face of the waters" (Genesis 1:2). The Spirit of God moved upon you and began to reveal Christ to you, just as the hormones stimulate the follicle to prepare an oocyte for ovulation. When Jesus Christ and the truth of God's Word was revealed, you were then faced with the choice of whether or not you were going to respond.

The Witnesses of Christ

According to God's Law, no one was to be condemned to death without the testimony of at least two witnesses:

At the mouth of two witnesses, or three witnesses, shall he that is worthy of death be put to death; but at the mouth of one witness he shall not be put to death. (Deuteronomy 17:6)

He that despised Moses' Law died without mercy under two or three witnesses. (Hebrews 10:28)

God has established many things that testify, or "bear witness" of Himself, but we find in scripture that there have always been at least two witnesses, even to those who have never heard the name "Jesus Christ." The first way that Jesus Christ—the Word, incarnation and literal expression of God—is revealed to every person is through the witness of *Creation*.

For the wrath of God is revealed from Heaven against all ungodliness and unrighteousness of men, who hold the truth in unrighteousness; because that which may be known of God is manifest in them; for God hath shewed it unto them. For the invisible things of Him from the creation of the world are clearly seen, being understood by the things that are made, even His eternal power and Godhead; so that they are without excuse. (Romans 1:18–20)

One of the most beautiful things in nature that illustrates the creativity of God is the birth of a child. It requires a far greater "leap of faith" to believe in a self- designed, self-created, and self-maintained universe than it does to acknowledge the existence of an omniscient creative intelligence. The odds against even the simplest of viral or bacterial life forms evolving "by chance" from primeval ooze—much less something as complex as you and me—are so astronomical as to defy comprehension. It violates all known laws of probability. Yet, the same educated people who smile condescendingly at the ludicrous medieval notion of *spontaneous generation* will defend this point of view. Why? Recall our illustration the ultraviolet light. Rather than condemning them, we must understand that their perceptions are based upon the "light" that they have; they do not understand that their light is actually spiritual darkness. Instead, we should pray that they will receive the true light which is Jesus Christ!

The second "witness" through which Christ has been manifested to every person who has ever lived is the God-given *conscience* within them.

> For when the Gentiles, which have not the Law, do by nature the things contained in the Law, these, having not the Law, are a law unto themselves: which shew the work of the Law written in their hearts, their conscience bearing witness, and their thoughts the mean while accusing or else excusing one another. (Romans 2:14–15)

God has given to every person some measure of discernment between right and wrong. There is no society on earth that has not had laws. Consequently, they are aware of when those laws have been broken. The problem we find with laws is our basic human inability to keep them. On the other hand, we see the consistency of God. He is obligated to observe His own Law; He cannot condemn anyone to hell without the testimony of at least two witnesses. When God gave the Law to Moses, He was fully aware of man's inability to abide by all of its provisions. Rather, it was given to illustrate man's need for something greater: *justification by faith*.

> But the scripture hath concluded all under sin, that the promise by faith of Jesus Christ might be given to them that believe. But before faith came, we were kept under the Law, shut up unto the faith which should afterwards be revealed. Wherefore the Law was our schoolmaster to bring us unto Christ, that we might be justified by faith. But after that faith is come, we are no longer under a schoolmaster. For ye are the children of God by faith in Christ Jesus. (Galatians 3:22–26)

The Law, then, was given to cause us to acknowledge our need for another means by which we could be reconciled to God. Thus, the promise of a "Savior" or "Messiah" was given; someone who would redeem us on the merits of faith, not on the basis of our own righteousness according to the Law. The price of our redemption was paid when Jesus Christ took our sins upon Himself and died on the Cross. The men of faith in the Old Testament looked forward to the Cross. We look back to the Cross and the fulfillment of God's promise. It was Abraham's *faith* that became his *righteousness* (Romans 4:3).

Two Ways to Heaven

In case you didn't know, there are *two* ways to get to heaven. What? Am I trying to propagate some strange new doctrine? No, there are two ways. Jesus said that one way is to "keep the commandments" (Matthew 19:17). Well, that just eliminated all of us. When we sin, we automatically break the Law and the scripture says that "*all* have sinned and come short of the glory of God" (Romans 3:23).

Well, what is the alternative? Do you recognize why Jesus Christ was raised from the dead? Because He kept the Law! If He had not kept the Law, you and I would be without hope of salvation. If He had sinned, He would have required His own redeemer. The only way God had of resurrecting Him was through perfect obedience to that Law. As a result of His obedience to God, He was able to purchase our salvation and provide a means by which we also might one day be resurrected to eternal life based upon the righteousness imputed to us through faith in Him:

> And if Christ be in you, the body is dead because of sin; but the Spirit is life because of righteousness. But if the spirit of him that raised up Jesus from the dead dwell in you, He that raised up Christ from the dead shall also quicken your mortal bodies by his spirit that dwelleth in you. (Romans 8:10–11)

As we indicated previously, God, in observance of His own Law, has always had at least two witnesses in the world. We have already mentioned Creation and conscience. In the Old Testament, two more witnesses were added: the *Law* and the *prophets*, typified by Moses and Elijah in scripture. During Jesus's ministry, He spoke of the fact that He bore witness of Himself and that the Father also bore witness of Him (John 8:18). When Jesus sent out his disciples in pairs, it was not that they might enjoy each other's company; it was to fulfill the Law! In the current "Church Age," which is characterized by *grace*, we find that Christ has again established two witnesses that testify of Him: the *Holy Spirit* and the *Church* made up of "born again" believers. In Revelation, we find the return of the two witnesses representing the Law and the prophets. Why? God is preparing to pour out His judgment—based on the Law—upon a wicked world that has rejected the dispensation of grace.

The scripture tells us that God is "no respecter of persons" (Acts 10:34). God is just, fair and does not arbitrarily esteem one person above another. We see the manifestation of this in our survey of the two witnesses. Every person who has ever lived on the face of the earth has had some revelation of Christ, even if it is only nature and the conscience within them. We must avoid the narrow doctrinal thinking that preemptively assigns a place in hell to persons throughout history who never heard the name "Jesus Christ." What rational human father would punish and disown his son or daughter for rejecting knowledge to which the child was not privy? More accurately, we know that every person will be judged based upon their response to the measure of revelation of Christ—i.e., truth, they received in this life. With the giving of truth, there is also the giving of accountability.

This brings us to the subject of you and me. Jesus said: "unto whomsoever much is given, of him shall much be required" (Luke 12:48). Based upon what we have studied thus far, it should be evident that those of us living in this generation have been given much in terms of our revelation of Jesus Christ. In addition to the manifestation of Christ in creation and in our conscience, we have the most conspicuous testimony of all: the *written* Christ—the Word— which contains the testimony of all of the other witnesses as well. Clearly, we are "without excuse." We have been called by God not only to be reconciled to Him through His Son, but to go and bring this Gospel, or "good news," to others. How is this accomplished?

The Path to Conception

Our little egg cell has thus far been unceremoniously dumped out of the ovary, rescued by the fimbriae, and now finds itself in the dark passage known as the fallopian tube. What now? If the oocyte could think, it would be reasoning: "Okay, here I am. Or, more appropriately, *where am I?* What am I doing in this dark, totally unfamiliar environment, cut off from all my companions back in the warmth and security of the ovary? I must be crazy! But if I miss the appointment with the sperm, I'll be one dead egg within hours! Well, I guess there's no turning back now. On the other hand, there's no going forward either. I don't have any means of propelling myself! Oh, great! What do I do now?"

Once again, nature mercifully intervenes as the hair-like *cilia* lining the fallopian tube, along with contractions of the tube itself, help to propel the oocyte toward the *ampulla*, the wide, curved portion of the tube where fertilization normally occurs. Meanwhile, the half-billion or so sperm just deposited on the cervix far below are facing their own dilemma. People frequently have the misconception that the sperm, since they have tails, simply swim up the uterus to search out the egg. In fact, most research suggests that the sperm are incapable of reaching the ampulla on their own. Again, intervention is required. Sexual stimulation sends a signal to the hypothalamus, which in turn directs the pituitary gland to release the hormone *oxytocin*. The resulting contractions of the uterus and uterine tubes help provide transportation for the sperm, in their seminal solution, to the fertilization site (figure 6).

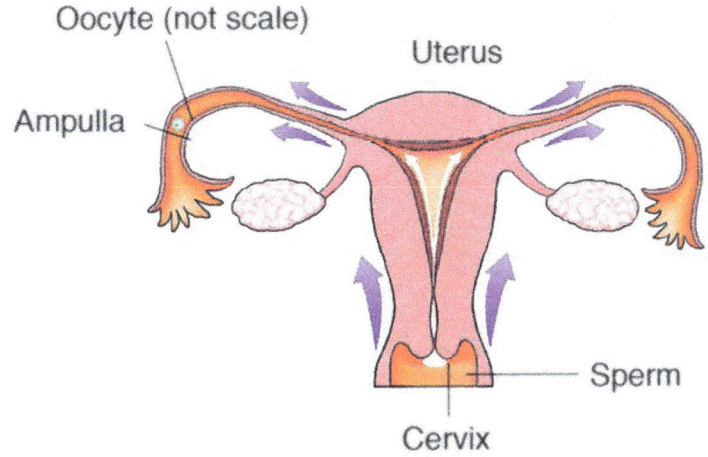

Figure 6. Oxytocin and Seminal Transport

Chapter 7 of 2 Kings in the Bible gives an account of four lepers at the gate of Samaria during a siege by the Arameans. They reasoned that either to remain where they were or to go into the city itself, where starvation was rampant, meant certain death. They concluded that the odds were at least slightly better if they defected to the invading army. They might be killed, but there was also a chance that they would be shown *mercy*. Upon arriving at the enemy camp, they discovered that the armies had abandoned the area and fled, leaving behind all of their equipment. They reveled in their newly acquired spoils until they recognized the wisdom of notifying the officials in Samaria. Their simple act of quiet desperation resulted in the fulfillment of Elisha's prophesy predicting the deliverance of the entire city.

Like the unfertilized oocyte that is abruptly launched into the abdominal cavity toward possible oblivion, the individual who makes the conscious choice to abandon the security of this world as they know it and entrust their future to a God they cannot begin to understand can face—from their point of view—a frightening prospect, but for which the only alternative is certain *spiritual* death. The decision to proceed itself may feel like it has death written all over it, but with this determination to pursue God at all costs—even through a "baptism of death"—there is great *hope*!

> Therefore we are buried with him by baptism into death: that like as Christ was raised up from the dead by the glory of the Father, even so we also should walk in newness of life. (Romans 6:4)
>
> Verily, verily, I say unto you, except a corn of wheat fall into the ground and die, it abideth alone: but if it die, it bringeth forth much fruit. He that loveth his life shall lose it; and he that hateth his life in this world shall keep it unto life eternal. (John 12:24–25)

Just as natural processes within the body provide all of the means for the oocyte and the sperm to come together during fertility, so God has made every provision for the salvation of a human soul. We have emphasized that God will do all that He can to draw a person to Christ, but there remains the element of choice or free will. God is a gentleman. He does not force anyone to love Him; He does not want "robots" or "puppets" for children. Very much like the oocyte, we were totally helpless to do anything about our spiritual condition before God began to draw us by the Holy Spirit. God chose, "while we were yet sinners," to love us. We, in like manner, must *choose* to love Him.

We will address the question of witnessing later in more detail, but Christians must be sensitive to what God is doing in the life of a lost person. Because of much improper teaching, we often get ahead of God in our efforts to see someone "saved." A person is not going to be genuinely saved unless he has been drawn by the Spirit of God. There is a very real danger in relying on emotional appeals to "convince" someone to accept Christ. Beware of those who employ cleverly devised "formulas" or "sales" techniques to bring people to a "decision." Until they have been convicted of sin by the Word of God and made aware of their darkened spiritual condition, people *can't* be saved! If they are not convinced that they are in danger of perishing, what are they going to be saved *from*? When lost persons are truly ready to die to themselves and live for God, you will not be able to drive them away with a two-by-four!

When the oocyte pops out of the ovary, it is totally committed; there is no turning back. Although the body sustains it, just as God will protect a person who is actively seeking Him, there is a limited period of time during which the egg cell can be fertilized. After about twelve hours, it will begin to degenerate and die. The ideal time for conception is when the oocyte is fresh, at the beginning of its passage through the fallopian tube. People often have the unscriptural notion that they can be saved at any point in their lives they may choose to designate. The scripture says, "Seek ye the Lord *while He may be found*, call ye upon Him while He is near" (Isaiah 55:6). Whether a person is sixteen or sixty, when God draws them finally out of the world toward an appointed time of salvation, they are going to have to go all the way with God.

> For He saith, "I have heard thee in a time accepted, and in the day of salvation have I [helped] thee: behold, now is the accepted time: behold, now is the day of salvation." (2 Corinthians 6:2)

Earlier we mentioned the fact that the Church and the Holy Spirit are witnesses of Jesus Christ. In Hebrews we find this admonition:

> And let us consider one another to provoke unto love and to good works: not forsaking the assembling of ourselves together, as the manner of some is; but exhorting one another: and so much the more, as ye see the day approaching. (Hebrews 10:24–25)

God expects His people to come together and to exhort and encourage each other so that His purposes may be accomplished through them. We find that the Church and the Holy Spirit work in tandem as believers are united and become "one" in the Spirit. Before they can be effectively used by God to pray and reach out to unbelievers, unity within the "Body of Christ" is essential. Many groups within the Church today are trying to promote "unity" at the expense of the truth, but what they fail to understand is that there can be no unity where there is false doctrine and compromise. Jesus stressed the issue of unity and truth as He prayed for His followers:

> Sanctify them through Thy truth: thy word is truth. As Thou hast sent Me into the world, even so have I also sent

them into the world. And for their sakes I sanctify Myself, that they also might be sanctified through the truth. Neither pray I for these alone, but for them also which shall believe on Me through their word; that they may all be one; as Thou, Father, art in Me, and I in Thee, that they also may be one in Us: that the world may believe that Thou hast sent Me. (John 17:17– 21)

Conception and Conversion

As we proceed, I think you will begin to find that the connection between the first birth and the second birth—and we should not really be surprised to discover that this is the case—is not only consistent; it is scriptural as well. Just as the hormones and sperm work in conjunction with each other to accomplish fertilization, so the Holy Spirit directs the Church to the unbeliever. As believers must work together in unity to carry the Gospel, so the sperm must be "unified" in seminal solution to reach the oocyte, providing us with a picture of the *Church*. As we will see, it is only the *nucleus* of a sperm cell that will actually combine with the egg cell to create a human being. The sperm, then, parallels the *believer* carrying the Word of God to the lost! The nucleus of the sperm, containing everything needed to make the oocyte "complete," is a beautiful picture of Jesus Christ, the Word, the *seed* of Abraham. What a profound correlation begins to unfold between the physical and the spiritual!

Our tiny oocyte is now approached by several dozen sperm that have managed to reach the fertilization site. The sperm then break up from their solution and begin to seek out the egg cell (figure 7). The oocyte is not simply penetrated by one of the sperm and fertilized immediately. Several things must occur first, including changes in the *lytic enzymes* contained in the head, or *acrosome* of the sperm. This is important because the sperm must first break down a layer of follicular cells which surrounds the oocyte. It is the release of enzymes from the heads of multiple sperm cells which enables one of the sperm to finally penetrate the *corona radiata* and a second layer known as the *zona pellucida*. It is passage through this second layer that produces a reaction which effectively prevents additional sperm from entering (figure 8).

It is highly symbolic that the sperm must first break down a resistant layer of cells before fertilization can occur. As it pertains to the unbeliever, this cell barrier represents *sin*. Before the Word of God can penetrate and bring life, the barrier of sin, unbelief and spiritual darkness must first be penetrated. Like the many sperm involved in conception, a number of believers may ultimately be involved—directly or indirectly—in the process of bringing a person to Christ.

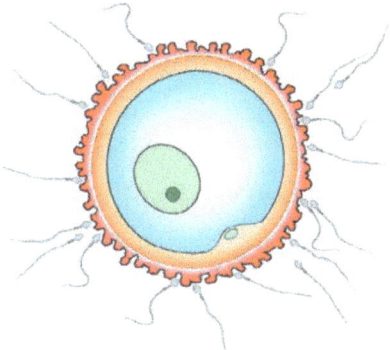

Figure 7. Sperm Assaulting Oocyte

In organic chemistry, the combination of two substances may not result in a reaction unless an *enzyme* is added. The apostle Paul wrote, "So then faith cometh by hearing, and hearing by the Word of God" (Romans 10:17). Faith is already present in the lost person, but it must be *activated*. The Word of God is an "enzyme" that activates faith and causes it to become alive.

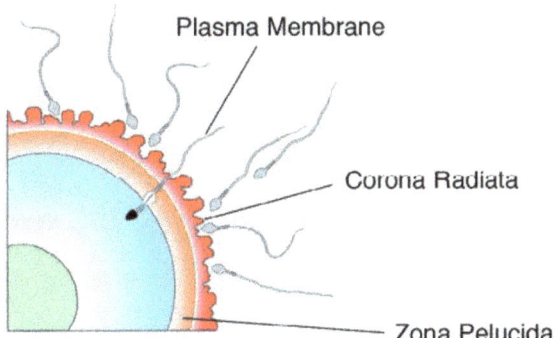

Figure 8. Fertilization

If the heart has become too hardened, the Word cannot penetrate. Faith, not activated, will then *die*. Paul says of his fellow Jews who had rejected the Gospel:

> For unto us was the Gospel preached, as well as unto them: but the word preached did not profit, not being mixed with faith in them that heard it. (Hebrews 4:2)

When a believer brings the Word to a lost person, it is *only* the Word that participates in the "conception." The believer is merely an instrument whose flesh is not a component of the salvation experience itself. It is significant, then, that the plasma membrane, or "flesh" of the sperm is left behind when the sperm penetrates the ovum. Ultimately, only the genetic material contained in the nucleus of the sperm will subsequently fuse with that of the mature egg cell, or *ovum*, to complete the fertilization process (figure 9).

The ovum, now fertilized, is much different than it was before the process began. The fusion of the sperm and the once "hopeless" oocyte produces a *zygote*, a single-cell conceptus in which are combined the chromosomes of both parents. Thus, it now has all of the *potential* to grow up into a full-term baby with some characteristics of both parents, yet with an identity all its own.

As we have already seen, when a person receives Jesus Christ as Savior, he becomes, like the fertilized egg cell, a "new creation."

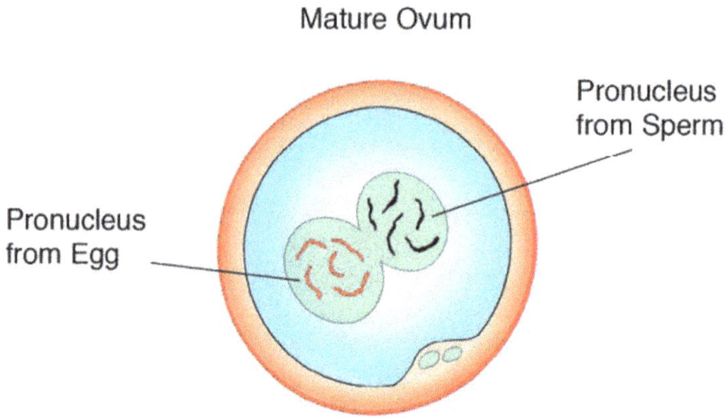

Figure 9. Fusion of Pronuclei (10 of 46 chromosomes shown)

> Therefore if any man be in Christ, he is a new creature: old things are passed away; behold, all things are become new. (2 Corinthians 5:17)

We previously referred to the fact that the new believer now has all of the potential to grow up into the "measure of the fullness of the stature of Christ." Like that oocyte in the ovary, he was once lost in darkness without life, without hope. Because he believed the word, repented of his sin and yielded his life to the unconditional control of Jesus Christ, he has now received God's Holy Spirit and has been "adopted" out of the world as a child of God. He has become "one" with Christ and is made a beneficiary of the hope and promise of eternal life. Like the conceptus which now contains the genetic traits of both parents, he now has two natures: the *flesh* and the *spirit*.

The Miracle of Salvation

I have seen a number of miracles during my lifetime, but to me, the greatest is the miracle that takes place when people genuinely receive Jesus Christ into their hearts and sin is forgiven! There is not a single thing a person can do in natural terms to be reconciled to God, but when God forgives sin, the slate is wiped clean! Satan, the "accuser," tries to point the finger and bring condemnation for past sins, but God checks His book and finds no record of them because they have been blotted out by the atoning sacrifice of the Lamb of God! Guilt is gone! This is why the apostle Paul was able to forget "those things which are behind" (Philippians 3:13). The sins he had committed as a result of misguided zeal prior to salvation were permanently covered by the cleansing blood of Jesus Christ shed at the Cross.

At the point of conversion, we receive a *new nature*. We now have within us the Holy Spirit who will give us understanding of God's Word and lead us in the way of truth. We receive the promise of God as Abraham did. Even though we are not "righteous," we receive the imputed righteousness of Christ based upon our faith in Him. In our lost state we were helpless to overcome sin. In Christ, we can now tap into the source of power over sin. Upon conversion, we are as pure and innocent as a newborn baby in the sight of God. Why? God is no longer looking at our flesh. Instead, He sees only that newly born spirit that has been made alive by the Word of God! He can no longer see our sin because we are now justified by the blood of Jesus!

It is important to understand that when we are "born again," we receive the hope of salvation and the promise of eternal life by *faith*. If we were to die immediately upon receiving Christ, we would then *possess* our salvation; there is no question but that we would spend eternity in God's presence. We must also receive God's forgiveness by faith. We cannot continue to dwell in the past. We could do penance from now through eternity and still not be able to repay God for what He has done. To continue living in self-pity and regret is itself sinful; it is *unbelief*. Instead, we must believe the promises of God and look forward to the finished product of our salvation.

> Being confident of this very thing, that He which hath begun a good work in you will perform it until the day of Jesus Christ (Philippians 1:6).

> Now unto Him that is able to keep you from falling, and to present you faultless before the presence of His glory with exceeding joy, to the only wise God our Saviour, be glory and majesty, dominion and power, both now and forever (Jude: 24–25).

Spiritual "Contraception"

We have seen a glimpse of the "glorious Gospel" of Jesus Christ. It seems almost incomprehensible that anyone would reject God's offer of eternal life and choose death instead. Yet scripture clearly indicates that most people—whether consciously or unconsciously—will make this choice. Why? There are a number of reasons, but let us begin with the following scriptures:

> And this is the condemnation, that light is come into the world, and men loved darkness rather than light, because their deeds were evil. For everyone that doeth evil hateth the light, neither cometh to the light, lest his deeds should be reproved. (John 3:19–20)

> The world cannot hate you; but Me it hateth, because I testify of it, that the works thereof are evil. (John 7:7)

Nightclubs and bars are characterized by very low lighting. What would happen if you walked into one and turned on extremely bright lights? The place would empty in no time at all. Lighting is frequently used as a deterrent to crime; most acts of human wickedness are committed under cover of darkness. One of the main reasons people do not come to Christ is that they love the things they are doing in "darkness," and they do not want them exposed by the light of Jesus Christ. Consequently, when the Gospel is presented, they stay as far away from it as they can.

Another reason people perish is that they will not take the time to search out the Word of God. A tragic scene will one day unfold at the judgment seat of God as many people who had Bibles lying on desks, coffee tables or gathering dust on shelves stand before their Creator. They are going to receive the sentence of hell and God is going to point to those dusty Bibles and say, "There was *life*…at your fingertips. But you never bothered to open it." They will be without excuse. Many of these people will have been drawn by the Spirit of God at one time but drew back and perished in the world.

Many people will perish under the misconception that they have "plenty of time" to get saved: "I've got a little more *living* to do." We have already seen that this is a fallacy. Even if it should happen to occur on their deathbed, there is an optimum time of salvation for every person. Others believe that they must somehow get "better" before they are worthy of coming to Christ. It will never happen; if we could get better, we would have no need of Christ!

Undoubtedly, the greatest reason people choose to reject Jesus Christ is the cost of *giving up control*. The irony of the "free" gift of salvation is that we must be willing to die to *self* in order to receive it. Also, Jesus promised persecution and suffering to all who choose to become His disciples. A common misconception among Christians is that "Jesus went to the Cross, so I don't *have to*." The fact is Jesus not only went to the Cross but also He commanded His disciples to follow in His steps.

> If any man will come after Me, let him deny himself, and take up his cross and follow Me (Matthew 16:24).

> Remember the word that I said unto you, "The servant is not greater than his Lord." If they have persecuted Me, they will also persecute you; if they have kept My saying, they will keep yours also (John 15:20).

It is possible, without drawing any conclusions whatsoever as to the relative merits or "morality" of birth control in its various forms, to observe some objective parallels between physical and spiritual "contraception." For example, in many parts of the world including the United States, there are either existing or impending legal and other "prophylactic" barriers which are designed to prevent Christians from spreading the Gospel. In some countries, a form of "spermatocide" is practiced where believers may be killed for sharing their faith. A type of "rhythm method" is suggested by any ongoing human or Satanic effort to thwart the convergence of a prepared heart and the Word of God. The birth control pill is a "counterfeit" hormone that prevents ovulation. Satan, in his determination to be like God, can emulate the activity of the Holy Spirit through religious "experience" and thus distract souls from being drawn by God. Like conception, *conversion*—the first step in the salvation process—can be inhibited by many factors. Ultimately, however, we will find that souls perish because of *unbelief!* Many people, for example, do not believe in the judgment of God. God's Law brings knowledge and awareness of sin, but most people do not believe they must *change*. In the ovary, there is little to distinguish one oocyte from another prior to ovulation. Because of peer pressure to conform, the security of "safety in numbers," and because most people don't perceive any difference between themselves and those around them, they see no *reason* to change!

A critical requirement for salvation is the conviction of, and sorrow for, *sin*. There must also be a desire to change. The word for "repent" in Greek is perhaps best illustrated as a military "about face." In counseling, I have met a number of people who will admit they have done things that are "wrong," but they are not ready to admit that they are in a rebellious state and need to *repent*. The mentality is: "Well, I'm a pretty good person." The worst thing you can do is try to convince a person in this state to make a "decision" for Christ. Their walk "with" God won't be any different than their walk without Him. You are not going to see a change until there is a brokenness for sin and a willingness to give up control of their lives to Jesus Christ.

When Jesus confronted His followers with the truth, many left Him. At times, He was left with only His twelve disciples. There is an element of pride in man that blinds him to the fact that he is a sinner in need of redemption. Or, if the Holy Spirit does bring conviction, he concludes that his sin is "justified." In any case, he certainly knows he is not deserving of *death*! What he fails to realize is that he is already *dead!* Is there still hope? Let us look to the scripture for the answer:

> Verily, verily, I say unto you, the hour is coming, and now is, when the dead shall hear the voice of the Son of God: and they that hear shall live. (John 5:25)
>
> For as the Father raiseth up the dead, and quickeneth them; even so the Son quickeneth whom He will. (John 5:21)

As we seek to understand the truths of God's Word, it is imperative that we search the scriptures for ourselves rather than being content with the doctrines and traditions of men. Having established a basis for the *salvation experience*, or spiritual "conception" of a human soul, our emphasis in the next section will be the aspect of "growing up" into Christ. In addition, we will more closely examine the topic of salvation and attempt to clarify the distinction between God's role and the role of the believer in helping to bring a person to Christ.

Part 2

Gestation: Growing Up into Christ

Fertilization has been accomplished, and as we have seen, the resulting *conceptus* now has all of the *potential* of becoming a full-term baby. It has not yet developed into the form of a moving, respiring, or recognizable human being, but all of the necessary components and the "blueprint" are present. When a baby is born, it must take that first breath in its new environment. If it does not, it was fully alive but never *possessed* its life independent of the life support system provided by the womb. A simple test can determine this. If a sample of lung tissue floats in water, then the baby took a breath. If not, the baby was *stillborn*.

When a person is born again by *faith*, or "conceived" in Christ, he or she now has all of the potential to grow up into the image of God's Son. Obviously, that person does not yet possess immortality in the literal sense, but they have the *promise* and the *hope* of eternal life on the basis of faith. Meanwhile, the process of "growing up" into Christ begins. When we receive Jesus Christ as Savior, we receive all of Jesus that we will ever have or need. Like the conceptus, all of the required elements and the "genetic instructions" are in place. In the words of Jesus, "It is finished!" In the beginning, a conceptus bears very little resemblance to its parents. Similarly, we as new believers don't look very "Christ-like" at first, but we have the Holy Spirit within us and all of the potential of becoming like Jesus!

For whom He did foreknow, He also did predestinate to be conformed to the image of his son, that He might be the Firstborn among many brethren. (Romans 8:29)

Beloved, now are we the sons of God, and it doth not yet appear what we shall be: but we know that, when He shall appear, we shall be like Him; for we shall see Him as He is. (1 John 3:2)

Sealed by the Spirit

When fertilization is complete, the conceptus (figure 10) begins an accelerated process of *mitotic* cell divisions known as *cleavage* (figure 11). By the time it reaches its destination and begins to implant in the uterine wall, or *endometrium*, it has already divided several times and is now at the *blastocyst* stage of development.

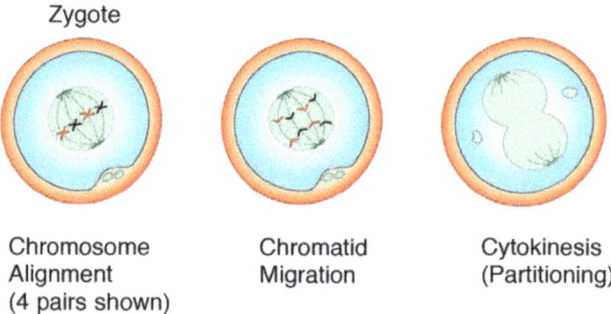

Figure 10. Phases of Mitosis (simplified)

Within a matter of days, it will have totally embedded itself within the endometrium.

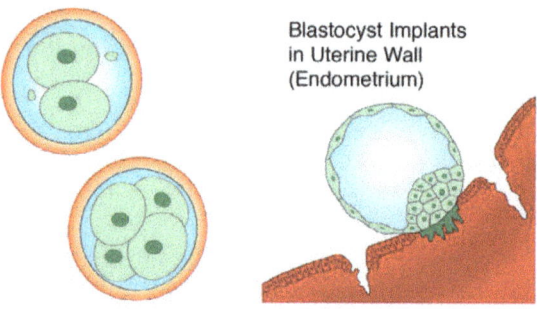

Figure 11. Cleavage (Mitotic Division) to Blastocyst Formation

The uterine lining, or *epithelium*, then closes back over the blastocyst so that it is literally "sealed" within the uterus. The scripture says that when we are saved, we are "sealed" in Jesus Christ:

> In whom ye also trusted, after that ye heard the word of truth, the Gospel of your salvation: in whom also after that ye believed, ye were sealed with that Holy Spirit of promise, which is the earnest of our inheritance until the redemption of the purchased possession, unto the praise of His glory. (Ephesians 1:13–14)

Paul warns against grieving the Holy Spirit, "whereby ye are *sealed* unto the day of redemption" (Ephesians 4:30). The *womb* is a picture of Jesus Christ! We find later that the growing fetus is literally sealed in the womb, not only within its amniotic sac, but also by a mucous "plug" which forms over the cervix. Just as the conceptus is sealed in the uterus during pregnancy, so the believer is sealed in Jesus Christ during the process of salvation. Spiritually, what is the evidence that I am *in* Christ? Paul writes, "For as many as are led by the Spirit of God, they are the sons of God" (Romans 8:14). In verse 16 of the same passage, he declares, "The Spirit itself beareth witness with our spirit, that we are the children of God."

Physically, how does the body "know" that it's pregnant? Previously, we have discussed the parallel between the relative functions of hormones and the Holy Spirit. When ovulation occurs, the collapsing follicle develops into a structure called the *corpus luteum*. It is the release of the hormone *progesterone* by the corpus luteum that signals the endometrium of the uterus to make preparations for the possible arrival of a blastocyst. If fertilization and implantation do occur, an outer tissue layer of the conceptus releases another hormone, *chorionic gonadotrophin*, which sends the signal, "We're pregnant!" to the ovary. Thus, resumption of the reproductive cycle is prevented. Subsequently, the *placenta* will produce hormones including progesterone which are necessary for pregnancy to be maintained.

Abiding in Christ

It is quite interesting to note that the implanted blastocyst, now a developing *embryo*, takes nourishment from the uterus by actively ingesting surrounding tissue and blood cells. It literally grows by "eating" flesh and blood until the placenta is formed, and it can be sustained directly by nutrients in the mother's blood supply. Do you begin to see what Jesus meant by the "hard saying" he delivered in the Gospel of John?

> Then Jesus said unto them, "Verily, verily, I say unto you, except ye eat the flesh of the son of man and drink His blood, ye have no life in you. Whoso eateth My flesh and drinketh My blood, hath eternal life; and I will raise him up at the last day. For My flesh is meat indeed, and My blood is drink indeed. He that eateth My flesh and drinketh My blood, dwelleth in Me, and I in him. As the living Father hath sent Me, and I live by the Father: so he that eateth Me, even he shall live by Me. This is the bread which came down from Heaven: not as your fathers did eat manna, and are dead: he that eateth of this bread shall live forever." (John 6:53–58)

The notion of consuming blood of any kind was anathema to the Jews, not to mention human flesh! Not only was the very idea abhorrent; it was a clear violation of God's Law! The problem was that Jesus was speaking in spiritual terms; his followers were perceiving with natural, human understanding.

Clearly, in retrospect, Jesus was referring to the fact that it is only by "feeding" upon the Word of God that our spirits will be nourished and have life.

Some observers believe that a whitish substance called *uterine milk* may serve a function in helping to provide nourishment to the conceptus in its very early stages of development prior to implantation. The apostle Peter admonished believers to "as newborn babes, desire the sincere milk of the Word, that ye may grow thereby" (1 Peter 2:2). Just as the conceptus must take nutrients from the mother in order to survive and grow, so the believer must continue to consume the spiritual "milk" and "meat" of Jesus Christ, the word, in order to grow up into His image.

Jesus said that we have been ordained to "go and bring forth fruit" and that our fruit "should remain" (John 15:16). Paul spoke of being "filled with the *fruits of righteousness*, which are by Jesus Christ, unto the glory and praise of God" (Philippians 2:11). As a branch must receive nourishment from the tree in order to bear fruit, so we must continue to "abide" in Christ in order to grow and bear fruit unto God.

> Abide in Me, and I in you. As the branch cannot bear fruit of itself, except it abide in the vine; no more can ye, except ye abide in Me. (John 15:4)

Dividing God's Word

Contrary to much popular teaching today, there are no "shortcuts" to a mature Christian walk, or a righteous, holy life. Regardless of the age at which we are saved, we are all born as spiritual "babes" in Christ. Many Christians aren't finding the joy and the fullness of God in their lives because they are not seeking Him with all of their hearts. Frequently, people have come to me and complained of their seeming inability to overcome sin in their lives.

I generally ask them, "Are you spending time in God's Word?" "Well, not *really*."

Some Christians are starving spiritually because their only meals consist of being spoon-fed by a pastor once or twice a week.

A new baby initially does quite well on mother's milk, but there will inevitably come a point at which its growing body begins to crave something more substantial. Large numbers of Christians are dying inside because they are sitting in churches where there is no substance, or nothing but salvation is preached, and they refuse to get into the scriptures and begin to seek God on their own.

After a certain length of time, children require solid food and must eventually learn to feed themselves. God will not force anyone to seek Him, however. If someone offered you a big, delicious steak and then put a gun to your head and told you to eat it, you wouldn't enjoy a bite of it, even if it happened to be your favorite meal!

As Christians, we must choose to fill ourselves with God's Word. As we spend time alone in communion with God and in the study and meditation of the Word, or *logos*, we are feeding our spirits the "bread from Heaven," the spiritual food made available to us through Jesus Christ!

> It is the Spirit that quickeneth; the flesh profiteth nothing; the words that I speak unto you, they are spirit and they are life. (John 6:63)

> Ho, everyone that thirsteth, come ye to the waters, and he that hath no money; come ye, buy, and eat; yea, come, buy wine and milk without money and without price. Wherefore do ye spend money for that which is not bread? And your labour for that which satisfieth not? Hearken diligently unto Me, and eat ye that which is good, and let your soul delight itself in fatness. (Isaiah 55:1–2)

A believer must learn to get "fat" on God's Word. If we were to feed our flesh the way most of us feed our spirits, we would be pitifully emaciated creatures indeed. In fact, we would starve to death! The more of God's Word you take in, the more you are able to trust God. The converse is also true: the less of God's Word you feed yourself, the more difficult it becomes to trust God. Why? "So then faith cometh by hearing, and hearing by the Word of God" (Romans 10:17). As you feed yourself with God's Word, it literally builds your faith!

God's Blueprint for Development

We have seen that the conceptus begins to grow by division. The "blueprint" for the growth and development of a full-term baby will be carried out as long as the conceptus remains in the growth process. It has all of the genetic potential to become a unique adult individual but is very unspecialized at first. With the exception of certain elongated nerve cells, the mature ovum is the largest cell that will ever exist in the developing human body. When fertilized, it doesn't just get "bigger." It grows by dividing and specializing into the various organs and structures within the body. Gradually, it will assume the form of a human being. How does the new believer begin to grow up into the full stature of Jesus Christ?

When we receive Christ, we receive His "genetic imprint" upon our hearts. God says, "I will put my Law in their inward parts, and write it in their *hearts*" (Jeremiah 31:33). The apostle Paul wrote that the believer is an "epistle" of Christ, "written not with ink, but with the *Spirit* of the living God; not in tables of stone, but in fleshy tables [tablets] of the heart" (2 Corinthians 3:3). If we are in Christ, we are no longer under the Law; the Law is now within us! We now have the potential to grow up into the image of God's Son. But since we receive all of Christ we will ever have when we receive Him, how do we grow? Paul wrote to Timothy:

> Study to shew thyself approved unto God, a workman that needeth not to be ashamed, rightly dividing the Word of truth. (2 Timothy 2:15)

Just as the conceptus grows by the process of mitotic cell division, so we must now "divide" the *Word of truth* and begin to build upon the foundation of Jesus Christ.

> For other foundation can no man lay than that is laid, which is Jesus Christ. Now if any man build upon this foundation gold, silver, precious stones, wood, hay, stubble; every man's work shall be made manifest: for the day shall declare it, because it shall be revealed by fire; and the fire shall try every man's work of what sort it is. If any man's work abide which he hath built thereupon, he shall receive a reward. If any man's work shall be burned, he shall suffer loss: but he himself shall be saved; yet so as by fire. (1 Corinthians 3:11–15)

Notice that, although our choice of "building materials" is not the basis for our salvation, the quality of our structure certainly has a bearing on our *reward*. Even though the doctrines of many people will not stand the test of God's refining fire, there will still be those saved "so as by fire" through the purification of their abiding faith in the foundation: Jesus Christ.

Clearly, there will be those, perhaps like the thief on the cross—whose revelation of Jesus appears to come at the very end of his life—who will barely make it into the kingdom of Heaven. They will have very little if anything to show for their second birth apart from salvation itself. As in the natural, there will be those born spiritually, as it were, with various "deformities" and evidence of stunted growth. In another context, Jesus indicated that it is far better to enter the kingdom of God "deformed" than not to enter at all (Matthew 5:29–30). But if we have been given the opportunity to build, why not choose to become as much like Jesus Christ as we possibly can? The scripture says that more will be required from those who have been given much. To walk with the hope that we might somehow squeak through the gates of heaven "so as by fire" is a dangerous way to live! Rather, why not desire the "abundant entrance" Peter spoke of?

> Wherefore the rather, brethren, give diligence to make your calling and election sure: for if ye do these things, ye shall never fall: For so an entrance shall be ministered unto you *abundantly* into the everlasting kingdom of our Lord and Saviour Jesus Christ. (2 Peter 1:10–11)

Building on the Rock

The development of a human conceptus (figure 12), particularly during the first eight weeks of gestation known as the *embryonic period*, is a subject of highly complex proportions. It is not within the scope of our study to examine this amazing process in great detail, but certain aspects deserve our consideration.

As if to accentuate the triune natures of both God and His own mirror image, *man*, the third week of embryonic development is characterized by the presence of three primitive aggregations, or *primordia*, of cell types known as *ectoderm, endoderm* and *mesoderm* which will divide and differentiate to subsequently form the many highly specialized organs and tissues of the human body, such as the brain, spinal cord, heart, bones, blood and muscles. In addition, we find within the embryo three distinctive cellular structures—the *primitive streak, notochord* and *neural tube*—which provide the basis for certain specialized cell production as well as the development of the vertebral column and the central nervous system.

As it grows, the human embryo goes through a series of fascinating structural folds and transitions that continually modify its shape and appearance.

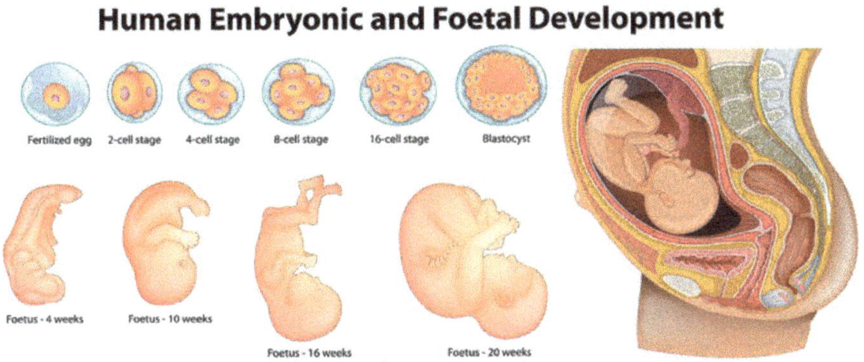

Human Embryonic and Foetal Development

Figure 12. Development of a Human Conceptus

For a time, it can be difficult to distinguish from the embryos of other species. Early on, it acquires appendage *buds*, which further specialize into arms and legs. These, in turn, begin to manifest tiny fingers and toes. A primitive but functional cardiovascular system is established during the embryonic period and various other components such as the digestive and respiratory systems are gradually differentiated as cells continue to divide, migrate, and become increasingly specialized. By the end of eight weeks, the embryo is decidedly *human* in its appearance. Guided by the complex genetic blueprint inherited in the chromosomes of its parents, the growing embryo is well on its way to becoming a full-term baby!

We have seen a brief glimpse of how a conceptus begins to grow into the "image" of a human being. How do we as new believers begin to grow up into the image of God's Son? We have seen that we must divide, or distinguish between, the various portions of God's Word and begin to build on the foundation of Jesus Christ. How is this accomplished? God is a God of *order*. Like the development of the embryo, we find that God's plan for causing us to grow up into Christ is a very *systematic* process.

Whom shall He teach knowledge? And whom shall He make to understand doctrine? Them that are weaned from the milk, and drawn from the breasts. For precept must be upon precept, precept upon precept; line upon line, line upon line; here a little, and there a little (Isaiah 28:9–10).

> But ye have not so learned Christ; if so be that ye have heard Him, and have been taught by Him, as the truth is in Jesus: that ye put off concerning the former [behavior] the old man, which is corrupt according to the deceitful lusts; and be renewed in the spirit of your mind; and that ye put on the new man, which after God is created in righteousness and true holiness (Ephesians 4:20–24).

If we are going to build, obviously we will need building blocks and mortar. What are the building blocks of "gold, silver and precious stones" Paul referred to? The traditions, experiences and "works" of men cannot be used to build upon the Word of God; these are the "wood, hay and stubble"! As it has been said, the only things in heaven made by man will be the scars on the glorified body of Jesus Christ. We are going to divide and specialize in the knowledge of Christ as we build with the *truths of God's Word.* These truths, or doctrines, will then be mortared into place by the *fiery trials of our faith.*

> Wherein ye greatly rejoice, though now for a season, if need be, ye are in heaviness through manifold temptations: that the trial of your faith, being much more precious than of gold that perisheth, though it be tried with fire, might Be found unto praise and honour and glory at the appearing of Jesus Christ. (1 Peter 1:6–7)

> Beloved, think it not strange concerning the fiery trial which is to try you, as though some strange thing happened unto you: but rejoice, inasmuch as ye are partakers of Christ's sufferings; that, when His glory shall be revealed, ye may be glad also with exceeding joy. (1 Peter 4:12– 1)

Experience vs. God's Word

Let us select a specific doctrine from the Word of God and use some illustrations to help explain just one of many aspects of the building process we have described. The Bible contains many accounts of *divine healing*, for example. One cause of illness described in the scripture may be linked to demonic forces, a "spirit of infirmity" that results from Satanic attack. When God reveals this as the cause, the spirit causing the illness can be rebuked and healing will result when faith is present. But the faith that God gives must be *acted upon*: faith without works (appropriate action) is "dead" (James 2:17).

One day, a young woman told me that her nephew had epilepsy and that the doctors were unable to help him. After she left, the Holy Spirit showed me that the problem—in this particular case—was a "spirit of infirmity," a *demon* of epilepsy so to speak, and that if I would call this woman and offer to pray for the child, he would be healed. I resisted, telling God that I couldn't go to someone and tell them their nephew had a "demon"! At that point, God brought to my mind the occasion described in chapter 9 of Luke when Jesus's disciples were unable to cast the evil spirit out of the young boy. Jesus rebuked the demon and the child was healed. I contacted the woman and read those scriptures to her. She brought the child to me, and as I approached him, he began to scream violently. I put my hand on him and commanded the spirit to leave in the name of Jesus. He was instantaneously healed. The doctors promptly decided they must have "missed" their diagnosis.

My awareness of a demonically induced illness was realized in another situation. My wife, pregnant with our second child, had an extremely high fever resulting from a condition that had not responded to prescribed medication. The Holy Spirit revealed to me that my wife's illness was the result of demonic assault. In Jesus's name, I rebuked the spirit responsible for the illness. As I did so, I began to run a high fever and suddenly felt terrible. My wife had been healed on the spot, but I realized that the spirit had attacked me instead. I again commanded the spirit to leave and immediately I recovered.

What can happen based upon experiences, like the two I have just related, is a tendency to believe that all illnesses are caused by demonic spirits and are Satanic in origin. That is the inherent danger of building a doctrine based solely upon an "experience," even if that experience can be validated by God's Word! Numerous maladies that afflict our physical bodies, such as allergies and a host of other health problems, may be hereditary and can be traced back to man's "original sin." The presence of disease-causing agents such as bacteria and viruses in our environment are also a result of "the Curse." People frequently carry unbalanced doctrines of healing to ludicrous extremes. I knew of a woman who kept trying to cast out the "demon" of cerebral palsy in her child. This was a congenital problem which had nothing to do with demonic activity.

We must understand that a truly born-again Christian can be assaulted by Satan, but he cannot be demon-possessed. First John 4:4 does *not* read, "Greater is He that is in *part* of you, than he that is in the *other part*"! Satan is often blamed for what is actually the result of *sin*. We should not discount Satan's role, however. In the case of the woman who had been confined to a stooping position for eighteen years, Jesus rebuked the "spirit of infirmity" (Luke 13:11). Clearly, there are Satanic forces with the power to afflict our flesh, if not our spirits. Contrary to the popularized notion of a comical creature in a red suit with horns, tail, and pitchfork, Satan has enormous power and is no less malevolent than he was in Jesus's time. Demonic possession among lost people is probably more prevalent in contemporary society than it was when Jesus walked the streets; it is merely diagnosed as a severe form of "mental illness."

To continue our illustration: I had seen illnesses that were caused by demonic spirits. My faith had been tested. The Word had been tested. Then, one day I was sick, and I rebuked the "spirit of infirmity." Nothing happened. I didn't get well. I realized that something else was wrong, and I asked God to reveal what it was. The scriptures admonish us to be reconciled to others before we approach God (Matthew 5:23–24). Also, we are to confess our faults and pray for each other in order that we "may be healed" (James 5:16). These scriptures came into my mind and God showed me that I had sinned against a brother-in-Christ, and that I needed to go and ask him for his forgiveness. I was instantly healed as this person prayed for me. There is scriptural evidence that illness can be the result of God's chastisement for sin. I had added another building block.

My aunt was dying of cancer, but I found that I could not bring myself to pray for her healing. Finally, God showed me that she, like King Hezekiah, had an illness "unto death" (2 Kings 20:1) but that prayer—in her case—would not make her well. She was ready to go home and be with the Lord! When I recognized that, I prayed that God would not allow her to suffer any longer. Within two hours, I received the news of her death. Paul told Timothy to use caution in laying hands on people. In our compassion, we tend to pray without asking God what He wants to do in a given situation. We need to learn to find the mind of Christ before we pray. It is time that we begin to grow into the full stature of Jesus Christ! I came to understand that a disease may be irrevocably terminal. Another building block had been put into place.

Our second child was born with both feet turned the same direction. The night before we were to meet with the surgeon referred by our pediatrician, God brought to my attention chapter 9 of John's Gospel, where the disciples inquired of Jesus regarding the cause of a certain man's congenital blindness. Jesus responded that his blindness was not the result of sin, but rather, in order that God might be glorified through his healing. It was revealed to me that this was the reason for my child's deformity. I "heard" the faith from God and I began to thank him that my son was healed for *His honor and glory*. When we woke up the next morning his feet were turned properly. Another building block!

God's Structural Test

Does God always reveal immediately the cause of illness and suffering? No! Job suffered for some time before he recognized that his faith was being purified as gold. As we begin to search out and build with the truths of God's Word, we are going to be tested. Those building blocks are going to be mortared into place through the fiery trials and testing of our faith. Some of the building blocks are going to be gold, silver, and precious stones. Others will be wood, hay and stubble. For example, Psalm 34:20 says of the righteous: "He [God] keepeth all his bones: not one of them is broken." Let us say that I happen to be late for work one day, so I "claim" this scripture and drive at twice the speed limit. I end up having a wreck and getting badly injured. Has God failed? Did His Word fail? No, I have foolishly tried to lay a building block that is highly combustible. The scripture says, "Thou shall not tempt the Lord thy God" (Matthew 4:7). It also instructs us to obey the laws of the land, which presumably include the posted speed limit. One building block has just gone up in smoke!

If we remain teachable, God in His faithfulness will put the test of fire to our faith and to our structure so that we don't end up with nothing but charred debris left on the foundation. If we are content to build with the doctrines and traditions of men, our building is already in serious trouble! You can't start laying brick on top of a layer of straw. Neither can we build on any foundation other than the Word of God. It would be foolish to lay a foundation of wood and then pour concrete on top of it. None of it is going to stand. As we grow in the knowledge of Christ and the truths of God's Word, those truths will be tested—as our faith is purified by "fire"—to make them a part of us. They must become a *reality* in our hearts and lives. As we learn to perceive and respond to life's circumstances in ways that glorify God we are gradually beginning to grow up into the full stature of Jesus Christ!

Many people think that we grow up into Christ by doing "good deeds." On the contrary, the good deeds are the natural result of a Christ-centered life. Others have the mistaken idea that life will be easy and trouble-free when they accept Christ. When they discover that this is not the case, many turn away. Jesus said, "In the world ye shall have tribulation," but in the same verse He said, "These things I have spoken unto you, that in Me ye might have *peace*" (John 16:33). When God's Word becomes a reality in your heart there is peace, no matter how difficult the trial.

When our third son was born, we were told that he would not survive a kidney malfunction. As I prayed, God gave me the scripture, "And whatsoever ye shall ask in My name, that will I do, that the Father may be glorified in the Son" (John 14:13). I *knew* when I prayed that my son was healed! I told the doctor, but they refused to release him from intensive care. Finally, when they tested him again and found that everything was normal, they allowed him to go home. The pediatrician wrote across his chart the word Miracle. This man went on to accept Christ and subsequently experienced a miracle of his own when he was healed of cancer through the power of prayer. Years later, he still remembered the peace God had given me at the time of my son's treatment.

Recall that "faith cometh by hearing, and hearing by the Word of God"

(Romans 10:17). Again, faith is a gift from God. When God speaks His faith into your heart through the Word, there is *peace* regardless of the circumstances! God becomes your focus instead of your problems. Many new Christians find that, at first, God seems to answer nearly all of their prayers—sometimes in miraculous ways—in spite of the fact that they haven't really learned to hear God's faith and to pray according to His will. This is the compassion and love of God. But God wants to take that immature faith and cause it to be refined and purified as we begin to grow and specialize in the knowledge of the Word, just as that new life in the womb continues to divide and differentiate into its many complex structures, organs, and systems!

Entering into God's Rest

By the beginning of the ninth week of pregnancy, the embryonic phase of development has graduated to the *fetal* period. By this time, all of the structures and primary organ systems of the conceptus are at some stage of development. The fetus, now easily identified as a human being, begins the dramatic growth process that will continue until birth and beyond as organs and tissues become increasingly specialized. Through the placenta and the umbilical cord—the "lifeline" which began to form weeks earlier—the fetus sheds waste products while receiving oxygen and nutrients from the mother's blood supply. Unlike its days as a blastocyst when it survived by actively ingesting the flesh and blood of the uterine wall, it is now attached and can simply "rest" and grow as it is fed directly by the mother.

God wants to have the same kind of intimate relationship with us through Jesus Christ. Once the foundation has been laid and we have become established in the basic doctrines of Christ, we can then begin to enter into God's *rest*. We continue to grow up into Christ and our faith continues to be tested, but we have finally learned that when we cease to strive and labor and begin to *trust* instead, then God is able to accomplish HIS purposes through our lives. The Bible speaks of the "Sabbath" rest of God. The Sabbath is a picture of Jesus Christ!

> There remaineth therefore a rest to the people of God. For he that is entered into His rest, he also hath ceased from his own works, as God did from His. (Hebrews 4:9–10)
>
> Come unto Me, all ye that labour and are heavy laden, and I will give you rest. Take My yoke upon you, and learn of Me; for I am meek and lowly in heart: and ye shall find rest unto your souls. (Matthew 11:28–29)

In order to enter into God's rest, we must first come to *know* Him. Many people are content to have an intellectual knowledge of God's Word. Their minds are stimulated by learning Greek and Hebrew. None of this will benefit them, however, without a knowledge of God's nature, personality, and character. We must seek to know Him—as Paul did—in the "power of His resurrection" (Philippians 3:10). Because you have read the autobiography of someone doesn't mean that you know them. You may have all of the facts about them, but until you spend time with that individual, you cannot honestly say you know the person. It is sad to see marriages in which the partners don't really know each other. They may be completely oblivious to the hopes, dreams, likes, dislikes, and emotional well-being of their mates. Genuine intimacy in marriage only comes through spending time together, opening up communication, and having the willingness to be vulnerable. It is the same way with God. He already knows your heart, but you must make an effort to get to know Him personally.

In the epistle to the Hebrews, the Jewish Christians were reprimanded for not being weaned from spiritual "milk" to solid food. They were encouraged to leave behind the elementary doctrines of the faith and press on to the deeper things of God. They were also warned against falling into the same pattern of unbelief that caused their forefathers to harden their hearts and perish in the wilderness rather than possess the land promised to them by God.

> Take heed, brethren, lest there be in any of you an evil heart of unbelief, in departing from the living God. But exhort one another daily, while it is called today; lest any of you be hardened through the deceitfulness of sin. (Hebrews 3:12–13)

> And to whom swore He that they should not enter into His rest, but to them that believed not? So we see that they could not enter in because of unbelief. (Hebrews 3:18–19)

How do we harden our hearts against God? If you aren't accustomed to manual labor, shoveling will produce a blister. If you continue to shovel, the blister becomes a callous. After a period of time, it can become so hard that you can stick a pin through it without experiencing pain. But in the blister stage, it hurts. It is the same way with God. If you continue to resist the Holy Spirit and the Word of God, your heart will become hardened. The more God speaks to you, the more you have to resist and the harder your heart becomes. The easiest time to deal with sin is when you are first convicted of it while the "blister" is still sensitive. The longer you resist, the more unmanageable your pride and rebellion become. Inevitably, our hearts become hardened when we refuse to obey the Word of God.

Throughout the scripture, it is clear the sin that most grieves the heart of God is not an act of our flesh. It is the sin of *unbelief.* Unbelief neutralizes faith, and where there is no faith, God cannot work. The scripture tells us that Jesus could not perform many miracles in his hometown because of the presence of unbelief (Matthew 13:58). Faith is not something you can work up by "claiming" scriptures. Remember, it is God's gift!

The fetus forming in the womb does not need any complex "plan of action" to cause itself to grow. It has no capacity to resist, to alter, nor to question the active process in which it has become a passive participant. It simply responds to stimuli as its internal blueprint unfolds. Our faith can only be exercised and grow as we simply trust God's Word and respond to His plan for our lives. Again, as growing believers, we must stand upon the promises of God and believe that He is able to complete the process of conforming us to the image of His Son. Hebrews 3:14 says, "For we are made partakers of Christ, if we hold the *beginning* of our confidence steadfast unto the *end.*" The only thing that can interfere with that process is unbelief. Hebrews 4:1 warns, "Let us therefore fear, lest, a promise being left us of entering into His rest, any of you should seem to come short of it."

Just as He promised a land of rest to the nation of Israel, God has promised a place of rest to you and me as Christians. You will recall that when Israel finally went into Canaan, there were still many battles to be fought; the inhabitants of the land, representing *sin*, had to be conquered. But it was God who fought the battles and defeated their enemies. As we enter into God's rest, the spiritual warfare of resisting sin will continue, but we recognize that in Christ we have the victory and the power to overcome!

God's Rest in Action

In this process of growing up in the image of Christ, *witnessing* is an important area in which many Christians have not learned to rest. Many feel that they have a sacred obligation to witness to every person they meet and are tormented by doubts and self-condemnation if they do not. When we cease striving to witness and let our *lives* reflect Jesus, then we can begin to enter into God's rest. We must simply make ourselves available and trust God to provide the opportunities for sharing Christ. If God doesn't open the door and prompt us by the Holy Spirit, we know that a person is probably not ready to receive God's Word. Jesus admonished His disciples not to "cast pearls before swine, lest they trample them under their feet, and turn again and rend you" (Matthew 7:6). There is a peace that should accompany our witnessing if we are truly being led by the Spirit of God.

Likewise, our prayer lives need to be directed by God. There is nothing inherently wrong with a "prayer list," but most Christians might as well make a recording and just push a button and play it back for God each night! The faith of many people is shaken when they pray without having direction from God and then find that their prayers are not answered.

> And this is the confidence that we have in Him, that, if we
> ask anything according to His will, He heareth us: and if we

know that He hear us, whatsoever we ask, we know that we have the petitions that we desired of Him. (1 John 5:14–15)

If ye abide in Me and My Words abide in you, ye shall ask what ye will, and it shall be done unto you. (John 15:7)

Clearly, if we pray according to the will of God, we can expect God to answer. Jesus said that He spoke no words unless they were His Father's Words. There are obviously things that we can pray for scripturally without a mandate from God, but the point is that we need to learn to wait on God and ask Him to reveal to us how we are to pray.

Many times, our prayers are outside of God's will because we respond to a perceived need in a person's life, but our prayer may be totally contrary to what God wants to do in the situation. There have been times when people have approached me requesting prayer for healing or other matters, and I have had to politely decline because I had absolutely no direction from God. There are no mental gymnastics you can do to build faith. We must learn to tarry at the feet of Jesus, resting and trusting in God until we receive His faith. Only then can we pray the prayer of faith. Five or ten minutes a day will not accomplish this. Prayer involves *listening*. A great man of prayer was once asked to describe his mornings spent in prayer. He directed the attention of the questioner to a prayer rug in front of his desk. He explained that he would lie face down in God's presence for three hours before any words were spoken. God ministered first to his spirit and then to his mind, so that when he finished praying, this man knew he had been in the presence of God.

Most of us will ask God to speak to us, but after five minutes, if we wait that long, we go on to other activities. God tells us to "be still, and know that I am God" (Psalm 46:10). If we wait before God in silence, it is astounding what can happen after thirty minutes or an hour. It took a long time to establish this "building block" in my Christian walk. There have been occasions when I have fallen asleep on my knees while in prayer. You may think that isn't very polite. It isn't! But sometimes it may be necessary to fall asleep with your spirit praying to God so that when you wake up your mind is clear and God can speak to you. At times I have fallen asleep while waiting on God and trying to pray, only to awaken and find God ministering and speaking to me. The scripture tells us that we will enter into God's rest when we learn to trust God and cease to trust in our own abilities. But until it becomes a natural part of our walk, we must "labor" to enter into that rest (Hebrews 4:11) by spending time in God's Word and prayer that we might come to know Him.

As you begin to spend time with God and in the meditation of His Word, He will reveal those areas of sin in your heart such as pride, jealousy, unforgiveness, anger and bitterness that must be conquered.

> For the Word of God is quick, and powerful, and sharper than any two-edged sword, piercing even to the dividing asunder of soul and spirit, and of the joints and marrow, and is a discerner of the thoughts and intents of the heart (Hebrews 4:12).

Although this scripture is certainly applicable to the unbeliever, it was written to Christians. In order to enter into God's rest, we must continue to "divide" the Word of God so that our minds become renewed, and we become more like Jesus in thought and action. Like that fetus attached to its mother by the umbilical cord, we can arrive at a place where we are resting in faith and totally trusting God without having to strive at it. I am told that Gandhi once declared that he might have become a Christian if he had never met one. Apparently, he was impressed with the claims of the Gospel, but never saw the reality of Jesus Christ in the Christians he encountered. It is a terrible indictment that many people can't see any difference between themselves and those who claim to be Christians. When we are totally sold out to Jesus Christ, people are going to see that there is something different about our lives. In Christ, we can overcome our tendency to respond as the world does.

> I beseech you therefore, brethren, by the mercies of God, that ye present your bodies a living sacrifice, holy, acceptable unto God, which is your reasonable service. And be not conformed to this world: but be ye transformed by the

renewing of your mind, that ye may prove what is that good, and acceptable, and perfect, will of God. (Romans 12:1–2)

Jesus said that we are to pray for our enemies and for those who take advantage of us. As Christians, we have died—by faith—to ourselves; dead men don't have any "rights." We cannot continue to feed ourselves on the trash of the world and expect to be different from the world. Sitting home watching pornography or movies and TV programs in which sin is glorified is not going to renew your mind in Christ. Instead, you will begin to think and act just like the unsaved!

The growing fetus doesn't have to *strive* in order to exist. It simply rests and grows as it receives oxygen and nutrients from its mother. As Mark 4:26–29 suggests, the farmer doesn't know *how* the plant grows; he just plants the seed by faith and waits for it to come to fruition. As we grow in Christ, feed upon the Word of God and cease to trust in our own works, we will find that God can begin to use us for His honor and glory. Like the growing fetus, we have an "umbilical cord," a spiritual lifeline called *faith* which connects us directly to the source of spiritual food: Jesus Christ! We become yielded vessels to God and soon find that, little by little, we are being molded into the image of God's Son!

The Natural Walk

There is nothing more *natural* than a baby growing in its mother's womb. As we grow up into Christ, our walk becomes, in the positive sense of the term, more and more "natural." A contrived, artificial "faith" that relies upon feelings and emotional stimulation is of no use in times of trial and difficulty in our lives. The scripture provides us with the proper perspective of a walk with God.

> The steps of a good man are ordered by the Lord: and He delighteth in his way. Though he fall, he shall not be utterly cast down: for the Lord upholdeth him with His hand (Psalm 37:23–24).

We must commit our steps to God each day and trust Him to direct our lives and to supply our needs. If we are worrying and striving over every obstacle, decision, and problem we encounter in our path, then we have not entered into God's rest. We lose our joy, and our lives can become filled with turmoil, disappointment, and anger. Instead, we need to simply learn to trust God.

> Therefore I say unto you, take no thought for your life, what ye shall eat, or what ye shall drink; nor yet of your body, what ye shall put on. Is not the life more than meat, and the body than raiment? Behold the fowls of the air: for they sow not, neither do they reap, nor gather into barns; yet your heavenly Father feedeth them. Are ye not much better than they? (Matthew 6:25–26)

God is intimately concerned with our everyday lives. Years ago, I was faced with a backed-up floor drain in my animal hospital. Determined to be my own plumber, I stubbornly tried everything I could think of, including hoses, plungers, and massive quantities of drain cleaner. Finally, I stopped and asked God to forgive me for not consulting Him. I then asked Him to show me what to do. He directed me to go into the next room, remove a brass plate from the floor, and put the hose down the opening. As I turned on the water pressure, a torrent of fetid, black sewage began to boil up from the drain through the standing water. My initial response was, "Oh, no! What a mess!" The question then came to my spirit, "Do you believe Me or not?" I replied, "Yes, Lord. Thank You for opening the drain!" Instantly, the drain opened up, and my problem disappeared. I previously had no idea that the brass plate covered a cleanout. But God knew!

Similarly, when God's Spirit begins to move in a person's life, the sin and refuse from the world must often be forced to the surface before God can clean up their life by the "washing of water by the word" (Ephesians 5:26). We should not be discouraged when our prayers and efforts to share Christ initially appear to bring a negative result!

Nowhere is a natural walk more important than in the area of witnessing. The salvation message itself is simple: "For whosoever shall call upon the name of the Lord shall be saved" (Romans 10:13). But how are people going to hear the good news of the Gospel? The apostle Paul continues,

How then shall they call on Him in whom they have not believed? And how shall they believe in Him of whom they have not heard And how shall they hear without a preacher? And how shall they preach, except they be sent? As it is written, "How beautiful are the feet of them that preach the Gospel of peace, and bring glad tidings of good things!" (Romans 10:14–15).

Every person who receives Jesus Christ as Savior becomes a *preacher*. Don't confuse "preacher" with "pastor." Unfortunately, in many churches, the pastor is also the only preacher. The pastor is supposed to shepherd the flock. It is the primary responsibility of the *sheep*, not the *shepherd*, to reproduce!

If I am a preacher, does that mean that I need to set up a soapbox on the street and "force" the Word into every person who passes by? Paul said that the life of a Christian is a written letter, or "epistle" (2 Corinthians 3:2). By our actions and our lives, we proclaim the Gospel of Jesus Christ. But we also need to "study" to show ourselves "approved" (2 Timothy 2:15) and be ready "in season" and "out of season" (2 Timothy 4:2) in order to effectively tell other people about Jesus. As we grow in Christ, we must learn to be good stewards of the Word of God. Many Christians go about indiscriminately confronting unbelievers with the Word of God because it will not return "void." It is important to note that Isaiah 55:11 says that God's Word will not return to Him void if He sends it out! That guarantee is not given to Christians who lack wisdom in their witnessing.

The greatest confusion associated with bringing people to Christ is a failure to distinguish between *God's* role and *our* role as believers. We must realize that only the Holy Spirit can bring conviction of sin and draw a person toward God. We must also come to understand that God is looking for availability, not talent. We don't have to be good-looking, gifted or educated to be used by God. Jesus's disciples were, for the most part, uneducated men. Observers were astounded when Peter and John preached in the temple. They could not understand how untrained, ignorant men could speak with such power and authority. The Spirit of God supplied the power and the authority; Peter and John were merely yielded vessels who desired to glorify Jesus Christ!

I tried witnessing to one of my clients for three years, but she would repeatedly cut me off. Two years after her final appointment, she came into my office and asked me to tell her about Jesus. I shared the Gospel, and she accepted Christ. She then asked me why I had never witnessed to her before! I just bit my tongue and rejoiced with her as she left my office with the joy of the Lord.

In another incident, my receptionist informed me that another veterinarian wanted to come by and see my hospital. I replied, "He's really coming by to get *saved*. But tell him he's welcome to come on by." Somewhat bewildered, she conveyed my invitation to visit, and I later gave the man a tour of our facility. He was preparing to leave when God reminded me that he had come to get saved. I had been waiting for an "opening" in our conversation, but none had appeared. As he started toward the door, I asked him, "Doctor, do you know Jesus Christ?" He responded, "Not the way *you* do." He received Christ and subsequently led his wife to the Lord.

God is looking for people who will simply listen and be available. How do we learn to walk "in the Spirit"? You can save yourself a great deal of money by not purchasing all of the books dedicated to this subject. The Word says that we are "in the Spirit" if the Spirit of God dwells in us (Romans 8:9). That's not too difficult, is it? We are in the Spirit by *faith*! We must continue to walk in that faith as we grow up into Christ. This is why our free will is so important; we must make the conscious choice to walk in the Spirit. Romans 8:5 says, "For they that are after the flesh do mind the things of the flesh; but they that are after the Spirit the things of the Spirit."

The desires of the flesh will never be satisfied. Instead of trying to accommodate our "dead" flesh, we must feed our spirits the Word of God. When we receive Christ, we do not lose our free will. We are still faced with the choice of yielding ourselves to the things of God or the things of the world. If we choose to feed our spirits with God's Word, we will find that our minds become renewed and the attractions of the world become less and less "appetizing."

For a truly born-again believer, it can gradually become quite a natural process to follow Jesus Christ in obedience. Jesus said, "My sheep hear My voice, and I know them, and they follow Me" (John

10:27). A pastor friend of mine was prompted by God to get in his car and drive out of town. He fought it because it didn't make any sense, but he continued driving. Just outside of town, he arrived at the scene of a serious automobile accident involving one of his church members. God wanted the shepherd present to minister to a hurting sheep!

There is a difference between having your ear "tuned" to hear God's Spirit and constantly needing to hear "voices." Many people have fallen into error because their entire walk with God is dependent upon a "word" from God coming either from an inner "voice" or through someone they regard as "spiritual." This becomes a very *unnatural* walk. Believers who have not been grounded in God's Word can become easy prey for satanic deception, because they lack discernment and cannot distinguish between God's Spirit and their own spirits or even between God's Spirit and demonic spirits!

Many people are also caught up in unbalanced "faith" doctrines because they don't distinguish between the "logos," the living, written, revelatory Word of God and the "rhema," the communicated Word of God given as directive to accomplish a specific purpose. When God speaks faith into your spirit, that is *rhema* from God. When my son was not expected to survive his kidney malfunction at birth, I was given rhema by God that he had been healed. God placed it in my heart; it was burned into my soul and spirit. There was no doubt in my mind that healing had taken place. Many people try to take the Bible and "claim" scriptures for themselves, but there is no faith because God has not spoken it to them. But when you hear rhema from God, it is as good as done! Just as the auditory nerves and the various structures of the ear gradually form in the growing fetus, so the ability to *hear God's faith* will develop in the believer who continues to abide in Christ!

It is important to recognize that our human tendency is to want a constant stream of rhema from heaven. However—although God may occasionally speak to us in direct and dramatic fashion—the natural walk demands that we consistently feed our minds and spirits the *logos*, the inspired words of God as contained in the scriptures from Genesis to Revelation. Often, the rhema is what we *want*; the logos is what we *need*!

The natural walk also applies to the area of *giving*. Beyond the scriptural realm of tithes and offerings to our local church, we are bombarded by the "needs" of people and ministries. We need God's wisdom and discernment in order to evaluate those needs. Some people may give too little because they aren't listening to God; others may give too much. We need to be able to distinguish between legitimate requests for assistance and the appeals of the multitudes of spiritual "bums" who make their living by exploiting the compassion of God's people. Paul wrote that, "if any would not work, neither should he eat" (2 Thessalonians 3:10). Jesus stated that if we are seeking God, our material needs will be supplied:

> But seek ye first the kingdom of God and His righteousness
> and all these things shall be added unto you. (Matthew 6:33)

It is one thing if a lay person is physically or mentally unable to work. It is an entirely different matter if he refuses to work or is indolent because he is "trusting God" to supply his needs through the Church. There are times when giving to certain individuals may just perpetuate their lost or backslidden condition. There are also many organizations that are constantly begging Christians for money. Many of these "ministries" are involved in doctrines or programs that have nothing in common with the Gospel of Jesus Christ. Whether it is a life or a ministry, we need to learn to discern the fruit of it. This is part of the natural walk. Unless we learn to hear God's voice, we may become very poor stewards of God's resources.

Within the heart of every truly born-again believer, there should be a growing desire to become more like Jesus and less like our old selves and the world. As John the Baptist said, "He must increase, but I must decrease" (John 3:30). As we have seen, it is God's desire to conform us into the image of His Son.

> And we know that all things work together for good to them that love God, to them who are the called according to His purpose. For whom He did foreknow, He also did predestinate to be conformed to the image of his Son,

that He might be the Firstborn among many brethren. (Romans 8:28–29)

Paul described the Galatian converts as his "little children, of whom I travail in birth again until *Christ be formed in you*" (Galatians 4:19). That tiny fetus growing in the womb has been predestined to look like its parents. Likewise, as the believer grows in the "womb" of Christ, he gradually begins to take on the appearance of God's Son. God did not save us so that we could go out and win the world to Christ. He saved us so that we could worship Him and have fellowship with Him. If we don't look very much like Jesus, how can we be an effective witness? If we establish a right relationship with God first, then people will begin to see Jesus in us, and we will become effective witnesses for Jesus Christ.

An Effective Witness

The remarkable ability of human beings to express abstract thoughts and ideas through complex language patterns is acquired through the interactive social learning process that begins soon after birth. The basic "wiring" for verbal communication, however, is established much earlier, during the embryonic stage of development. The *innervation* of the growing conceptus is accomplished by the intricate development of the *nervous system*, which consists of the *central* nervous system (the brain and spinal cord), the *peripheral* nervous system (sensory nerve cells, or *neurons*, emanating from the central nervous system to the various parts of the body), and the *autonomic* nervous system (nerves that control involuntary body functions). Research indicates that the processing of language takes place primarily in the left side of the brain; the peripheral nervous system includes *cranial nerves*, which branch out from the *medulla* to provide connections to all of the structures—including the eyes, ears, facial muscles, larynx, and tongue—that enable us to perceive as well as to communicate our thoughts and feelings to those around us. But the ability to communicate *effectively* is a process that requires time and learning.

Witnessing is a form of communication, but God has a methodology for the spiritual just as he does for the physical. One of the most beautiful examples in scripture of an effective witness is found in chapter 8 of Acts, where we find the account of Philip's encounter with the Ethiopian eunuch. The Holy Spirit interrupted Philip in the middle of a great preaching crusade in Samaria and told him to go to the desert. Can you imagine this happening to one of our well-known TV evangelists? Would he go? Would I go? Can you hear Philip saying, "But Lord, look at all of the people who are being saved and healed through *my* ministry! And you want me to go down into the desert? Besides, there's nothing down there but snakes and lizards; certainly not enough people to make the trip worthwhile!"

Unfortunately, we tend to measure "success" by man's standards. Philip didn't argue with God. He obeyed and went down into the desert. What did he find? Here was a man who was "ripe" for salvation. He had traveled many miles to Jerusalem to worship. There he had seen all the wonders of the temple and the many trappings of *religion*, but he had not met Jesus Christ...*yet*. On his way back to Ethiopia, he just "happened" to be reading scriptures in Isaiah that prophesied of the Messiah. He was seeking God with all of his heart! Philip merely walked through a door that God had already opened. The eunuch was gloriously saved in the middle of nowhere! He even got to see a miracle as Philip was "transported" to another location. Although Philip was being used in a supernatural way, his was a natural walk that resulted from a Christ-centered life. Although our witnessing experiences are seldom this dramatic, we should have the same kind of sensitivity to the Spirit of God that Philip had.

God intended for us not only to have fellowship with Him but also with our brothers and sisters in Christ. The scripture tells us that it is our *love* for one another that will identify us as God's children. It is not being hit over the head with a Bible that brings someone to Christ. It is the love he can see in the lives of professing Christians. You don't have to tell a lost person that he is a "sinner"; he already knows that. The best illustration I know of is that of a skinny, underfed mongrel dog with his dry bone. That dusty old bone doesn't have a shred of protein left on it, but it's all he's got! If you try to grab it out of his mouth, he'll take your arm off! But if you offer him a big, juicy steak instead, he'll drop that bone in a hurry!

Similarly, there is that neighbor down the street with his feet propped up on the coffee table, finishing his six-pack. It's all he's got! If you tell him, "Get rid of that!" you'll have a fight on your hands! But if the Holy Spirit and the Word of God can ever convince him that there is much more "gusto" in Jesus, he'll forget all about that six-pack and come to Christ. Maybe not overnight, but he will come. I'm not suggesting that there will not be times that you may need to gently confront someone with a drinking problem. I'm talking about the person who doesn't know Christ. You don't have to tell them that it's wrong: "You're going to hell if you don't stop getting drunk!" That's bringing *condemnation* instead of coming with the attitude that you know someone (Jesus) who can help them learn to *really* live!

After I came to Christ, I could honestly say that I drank all I wanted; I just didn't *want* to drink anymore. I smoked all I wanted; I just didn't *want* to smoke anymore. God gives you something better. Our tendency is to focus on the sin and say, "You're sinning. You've got to stop it!" "Look, if I could stop it, I *would*. But I *can't*!" We must introduce them to the One who can give them a new nature and the power to overcome sin. When we have a right relationship with God, then we can have a right relationship with our fellow Christians. In turn, the unsaved can see the reality of Jesus in the body of Christ. Everyone wants to be loved. They will be drawn to that love if they can see Jesus in the life of the believer. We can then be used as effective witnesses.

In scripture, children are sometimes referred to as the "fruit of the womb." We come to see that spiritual fruit in the life of the believer is a very significant aspect of growing up into the image of Christ. Paul writes concerning this fruit:

> But the fruit of the spirit is love, joy, peace, longsuffering, gentleness, goodness, faith, meekness, temperance: against such there is no law. And they that are Christ's have crucified the flesh with the affections and lusts. If we live in the Spirit, let us walk in the spirit. (Galatians 5:22–25)
>
> Herein is My Father glorified, that ye bear much fruit; so shall ye be My disciples. (John 15:8)

There is no way that we can develop these attributes on our own. Instead, we must receive Christ and, by faith, trust God to manifest them in our lives. Notice that it is the fruit of the *Spirit*. It is not the fruit of our flesh or our good intentions or even our good deeds. We begin to grow into these attributes only as we yield ourselves in obedience to the Word of God. We cannot love the unlovely, for example. But Jesus can, *through* us. Our selfish, controlling nature must be sacrificed in order for us to become vessels that will glorify God. As witnesses of Jesus Christ, we have two primary responsibilities: to pray and to proclaim God's Word. As we mentioned earlier, much confusion about witnessing has to do with the failure to distinguish between God's role and our role as believers. We must understand that we are not expected to "save" anyone. Only God can do that. Neither can we cause someone to be "drawn" to Christ. We may be used as an instrument, but only the Holy Spirit can accomplish this. Our lives will be evaluated by God, not on the basis of the number of people we have "won" to Christ, but rather on the basis of our faithfulness and obedience to His Word.

The sad fact is that there are going to be many people who will never accept Jesus Christ. If I am not hearing from God and being led by Him, I may spend endless hours witnessing and ministering to people who have no intention of ever seeking God. Instead, we need to be sensitive to the Holy Spirit so we know when it is time to "shake the dust off our feet" and go on. In our own strength, we will begin to strive and allow human compassion to interfere. We may even start looking for signs of salvation where there are none.

Discretion is compulsory in our efforts to share Christ with those who know us best—i.e., the members of our own families. Jesus spoke of the fact that a prophet was not without honor except among his own people. Unfortunately, our families are more easily reminded than others of what we were like prior to salvation. With parents, siblings, and offspring, our actions and attitudes invariably invite much more consideration than our words. Several years of "damage control" were required to heal the alienation I caused with certain members of my family resulting from zeal without wisdom in my early Christian walk. God may provide an opportunity for us to share Christ with our relatives, but even if He can't use us, He is certainly more than able to send someone else to them. Meanwhile, I just need to be faithful doing what God has called me to do where I am. We must entrust our lost relatives to God!

No Respecter of Persons

If you were to ask me how I treat people, I would respond, only *half*-jokingly, that "I treat everybody like they're *lost!*" What do I really mean by this? I spent five years thinking I was saved when I wasn't. I would minister to people and see them come to Christ, finding myself longing for the joy and peace I could then see in them. I have also ministered to many people who—for various reasons— had always "assumed" that they were saved, only to realize their lost condition. Consequently, I always try to be sensitive to the Spirit of God. If God impresses me to share scriptures on salvation with someone, I do it, even if it's someone in the ministry! A seminary professor with a PhD and a ThD once came to me, and I shared the Gospel with him. He looked at me and said, "I wish I had the joy you have." Even though he had great intellectual knowledge of God's Word, there was an absence of any spiritual understanding, joy, or peace in his life. Why? He had never been born again. I felt great compassion for the man because I had been in his shoes.

We should never simply assume that another person is born again solely on the basis of their appearance, conversation, or behavior; no matter how "spiritual" they may seem outwardly. If we draw this conclusion, we may miss an opportunity to be used by God. Many people think they are saved, as I did, on the basis of some religious "experience" they had years ago. In working with drug addicts, I have seen a number of them get genuinely saved, but I have met others who had encountered the angel of light, Satan, while on a drug trip and believed they had met Jesus Christ! I have also seen people who had been miraculously "delivered" from a demonic drug addiction, only to receive a Satanic religious spirit of self-righteousness in its place. We should not underestimate Satan's power to blind people to the truth.

> But if our Gospel be hid, it is hid to them that are lost: in whom the god of this world hath blinded the minds of them which believe not, lest the light of the glorious Gospel

of Christ, who is the image of God, should shine unto them. (2 Corinthians 4:3)

> When any one heareth the Word of the kingdom, and understandeth it not, then cometh the wicked one, and catcheth away that which was sown in his heart. This is he which received seed by the wayside. (Matthew 13:19)

We have mentioned the responsibility of the believer to pray for the unsaved. We need to be led by the Spirit of God in this area as well. The scripture tells us that "the effectual fervent prayer of a righteous man availeth much" (James 5:16). As we have seen, when we pray according to God's will, we can be confident of the answer. There may be situations in which we do not have the freedom to openly share Jesus, but God can still use our prayers to intervene in the life of an unsaved person. Prayer is done in the "trenches." Some people are eager to witness but neglect their responsibility to pray. As we have indicated previously, we must not be dismayed by the results when we pray for people and it seems that things in their lives go from bad to worse. Many people will not cry out to God until they have "bottomed out" in the depths of their sin. It may be only through considerable suffering that they will ever acknowledge their need for God. We must be especially careful in such cases that in our human compassion, we don't try to pray them out of their circumstances. If we are not hearing God, we may even help to perpetuate their lost condition by failing to discern the true need in their lives.

Since God is no respecter of persons, He cannot just "save" someone without showing partiality. In order that He may intervene in the lives of lost people, He is constantly looking for those believers who are willing to pray and intercede on their behalf.

> And I sought for a man among them, that should make up the hedge, and stand in the gap before Me for the land, that I should not destroy it: but I found none. (Ezekiel 22:30)

There were several occasions when God would have destroyed Israel in the wilderness had it not been for the intercession of Moses. We must not discount the importance of our prayers; there is evidence that God can actually "store" them until they are needed (Revelation 5:8). Not only does God use our prayers to begin to draw people to Christ, but there have been many documented cases in which human life was actually spared because someone was sensitive to pray.

There are any number of books available on the topic of "leading" people to Christ. We must understand that God has only called us to pray and to proclaim the Gospel. It is God's responsibility to draw people to Christ and to save them. God is not going to hold us accountable for the results; He is much more concerned with our *obedience*. There was a time in my early Christian walk when I would take people through a salvation "plan" and then ask them, "Is there any good reason you shouldn't accept Jesus Christ as your Lord and Savior?" Of course, I had just told them they were going to *hell* if they didn't! What person in their right mind would refuse to recite some glib "repeat after me" prayer formula if there was even a remote chance it could spare them the agony of being tormented in hell for eternity? No one wants to appear stupid!

None of this is intended to discount the reality that many sincere people have received Christ at a time when they may have recited someone else's prayer; we find that God's grace many times covers the mistakes we make and the habits we acquire in our zeal as new Christians. But God wants us to grow up! I had led a number of people through a "sinner's prayer," only to see a look of bewilderment on their faces afterward and the absence of any joy or peace in their lives. I suspected that something was wrong. One day in our office, an associate and I prayed with a man to receive Christ. When he left, I knew the man was not saved and I indicated this to my associate. He responded, "Well, he prayed the sinner's prayer. He *must* be saved!" But deep inside, I was certain that no change had taken place. Sure enough, six months later the man returned to our office with the joy of the Lord written all over his countenance. He thanked us and declared, "You guys really stirred me up! I started going to church, and I want you to know that last Sunday night I accepted Christ." My suspicions were confirmed. Needless to say, we had to reevaluate our approach to witnessing.

One of my children came to me one day and asked me to explain salvation. I sat down with him and went through the scriptures. When I finished, he just sat there and didn't say anything. I asked him if he had any questions and he responded, "Can you fix my bike?" I had just shared Christ with him, and all he could think about was his bicycle! We made the repairs, although—like the tire on his bicycle—I was somewhat deflated. That night, after everyone else had gone to bed, he came into my study and asked if I would explain salvation to him one more time. I reviewed the Gospel a second time, and he promptly declared that he wanted to receive Jesus. He prayed on his own without any assistance from me. When he finished, I asked him where Jesus was in relationship to him, and he responded, "Daddy, He's in my heart!" How did he know? "Because I *asked* Him to come in. And the Bible says that if I *ask* Him, He *will*. And He *did*. I KNOW He did!"

There are certain hormonal and physical conditions that must be present in the woman's body in order for conception to take place. For salvation to occur, a person must first be drawn by the Holy Spirit. He can then recognize his lost state and be convicted of sin. His faith must then be "activated" by the Word of God. If this has not occurred, he can ask Jesus to save him all day long and nothing will happen! We must avoid the notion that if I can't "convince" someone to receive Christ immediately, he might be hit by a car and perish in his sin! This is not trusting God. God is certainly impartial, but if a person is actively seeking Him, there is a certain amount of protection in that seeking. It may be years before he is saved, but God is more than able to keep him until that day arrives. We need to let *God* save people! It is much easier to lead someone through a "one-size-fits-all" prayer ritual than it is to intercede and struggle with them through the labor pains that are often necessary before someone is ready to be born into the kingdom of God. You and I don't know who is and who is not ready to receive Christ. God does. We must do our part to pray and proclaim the Word and then trust God with the results!

> Who then is Paul, and who is Apollos, but ministers by whom ye believed, even as the Lord gave to every man? I have planted, Apollos watered; but god gave the increase. So then

neither is he that planteth anything, neither he that watereth; but God that giveth the increase. (1 Corinthians 3:5–7)

But by the grace of God I am what I am: and His grace which was bestowed upon me was not in vain; but I laboured more abundantly than they all: yet not I, but the grace of God which was with me. (1 Corinthians 15:10)

Jesus's parable of the sower in chapter 4 of Mark helps to illustrate the importance of soil preparation prior to planting. There is the seed that falls by the "wayside." This ground represents those people whose hearts have not been prepared at all. They have not yet been drawn by the Holy Spirit. They hear the Word, but it just lies there, exposed. It cannot penetrate the uncultivated soil and Satan quickly comes and takes it away. Then there are those who *receive* the Word, but complications arise when trials and the cares of the world—the stones and the thorns—overwhelm them.

Each spring, the first order of business on the farm where I was raised was to remove the rocks from the fields. There were two reasons. Obviously, crop yield is reduced in rocky soil. The other reason was that rocks tear up machinery in very short order. The next thing we did was to get rid of the weeds and thistles *before* we sowed the grain. The point is God expects us to be good stewards of the Word. He is able to extract those stones and thorns from the life of a new believer, but how much better if those obstacles to God's Word can be exposed prior to planting! Sometimes people need to spend more time in the world before they are ready to receive God's Word. In order to be effective laborers in the harvest, we must recognize that our part is to sow, water, and assist in the cultivation. It is God's part to produce the harvest!

It should be very apparent that God wants to see people saved a lot more than we do. But we must be sensitive to God's methods. There will be many situations in which you will just have to be a friend to someone in order to "win" the right to share the Gospel. It may be years before God opens that door. In the meantime, however, you can be assured that they are observing your life and behavior. As "written epistles," our *lives* are much more credible than our spoken words!

Many people have told me that they didn't really understand salvation until after they were saved. Why? Until you are saved, you don't have the Holy Spirit to bring full understanding of God's Word. You can only understand that you have a *need* of salvation. In our witnessing, we need to remind ourselves that a lost person cannot understand the things of the Spirit of God. When I graduated from veterinary school, I had a tendency to communicate with confusing medical terminology. We as Christians often do the same thing when we use the vernacular of "Christianity" in our witnessing. We don't have to make it complicated. Instead, we must be sensitive as Jesus Christ perceives the need in a person's life. He will show the Holy Spirit, who will in turn reveal it to them.

Jesus didn't minister to every person He passed on the streets. There were many people in need of healing at the Pool of Bethsaida; Jesus healed only one man. Does this mean that God is a respecter of persons? No, Jesus was simply perceiving who was and who was not ready to receive the Word of God. The words that He spoke were *God's* words. The works that He performed were *God's* works. Just because we perceive a need does not necessarily mean that God is telling us to try to meet that need. We need to learn, as Jesus did, to hear God's voice so that we can be directed to those people God wants to touch. We have a tendency to respond based upon outward appearance. God, meanwhile, is looking at the heart!

The Body of Christ

The nine-month gestation period of the typical pregnancy is frequently divided into three *trimesters* of approximately equal duration. As we have indicated, all of the structural and systemic components that constitute a physical human being are in place by the ninth week. All internal organs are substantially developed by the end of the first trimester and, from this point, gestation is largely a matter of maturation and growth. By the end of the second trimester, the last remaining obstacle to viability—the ability of the fetus to survive outside of the uterus—is usually the respiratory system. The third and final trimester, however, is characterized by increasing odds of viability as the lungs continue to develop, as well as by a dramatic increase in the amount of fetal body fat. By the end of thirty-eight weeks and completion of the final trimester, the fetus has reached full term. The next major development will be the live birth of a new baby boy or girl!

Others have written extensively regarding the spiritual symbolism of various aspects of human physiology, including such topics as the circulatory and central nervous systems. It is not our intention to elaborate on their observations. However, let us examine what one writer had to say about the amazing process we have just described.

> I will praise Thee; for I am fearfully and wonderfully made: marvelous are Thy works; and that my soul knoweth right well. My substance was not hid from Thee, when I was made in secret and curiously wrought in the lowest parts of the earth. Thine eyes did see my substance, yet being imperfect; and in Thy book all my members were written, which in continuance were fashioned, when as yet there was none of them. (Psalm 139:14–16)

In the course of conception and gestation, we can see the incredible metamorphosis of a single, helpless *cell* into a human being that looks something like its parents (in most cases). Similarly, through the process of salvation we can observe the remarkable transformation of a single, helpless *soul* into a spiritual being that resembles Jesus Christ! David's wide-eyed amazement at God's handiwork in Psalm 139 speaks not only to the physical, but to the spiritual as well!

As a believer, I become a "temple" of God's Holy Spirit (1 Corinthians 6:19). But as followers of Christ, we do not only grow up individually into the image of Christ; as we are joined to other believers by our common faith, we are building and growing *corporately* as well. Peter writes that we are a "holy priesthood," "lively stones" in God's "spiritual house" (1 Peter 2:5). Collectively, we become the *bride* of Jesus Christ, who is the "chief cornerstone" of this eternal edifice (1 Peter 2:6). Together, we constitute the *Body of Christ*, better known as the Church! In order to facilitate this corporate growth process, God has established certain *ministries* within this spiritual structure.

> And He gave some, apostles; and some, prophets; and some, evangelists; and some, pastors and teachers; for the perfecting of the saints, for the work of the ministry, for the edifying of the Body of Christ: till we all come in the unity of the faith, and of the knowledge of the Son of God, unto a perfect man, unto the measure of the stature of the fullness of Christ (Ephesians 4:11–13).

Each individual believer constitutes a member of the body of Christ. Participation in this sacred assembly is not optional for a Christian; recall the admonition in Hebrews that we are not to neglect the "assembling of ourselves together." There is not one member of the body that is more important than the others. The Church provides not only a haven for the instruction and encouragement of its members, but protection for them as well.

> That we henceforth be no more children, tossed to and fro, and carried about with every wind of doctrine, by the sleight of men, and cunning craftiness, whereby they lie in wait to deceive; but speaking the truth in love, may grow up into him in all things, which is the head, even Christ: from whom the whole Body fitly joined together and compacted by that which every joint supplieth, according to the effectual working in the measure of every part, maketh increase of the Body unto the edifying of itself in love (Ephesians 4:14–16).

It is interesting to note that in the human male body, the urogenital system is directly tied to the reproductive system. A common channel is shared by the part that eliminates waste and the part given the greatest "honor"—i.e., the reproductive function. This illustrates the significance of Paul's statements to the Corinthians:

> But now hath God set the members everyone of them in the Body, as it hath pleased Him. And if they were all one member, where were the Body? But now are they many members, yet but one Body. And the eye cannot say unto the hand, "I have no need of thee": nor again the head to the feet, "I have no need of you." Nay, much more those members of

the Body, which we think to be less honourable, upon these we bestow more abundant honour; and our uncomely parts have more abundant comeliness. For our comely parts have no need: but God hath tempered the Body together, having given more abundant honour to that part which lacked. (1 Corinthians 12:18–24)

God has placed us in the Church, and it doesn't make any difference what we think of ourselves. Those members who appear outwardly to be the least gifted or the most unattractive may be the very ones used by God in the greatest ways. When Jesus chose His disciples, did He go to the religious or social elite? No! With the exception of Luke the physician, He chose men such as tax collectors and fishermen who were largely uneducated and at the bottom of the social hierarchy. Yet they were mightily used by God!

At one time, the most important qualification for a clergyman was the call of God. Today, unfortunately, the emphasis has turned to academic background, personal "charisma" or impressive oratory. Instead of being encouraged to hear from God through His Word, many Bible school and seminary students are being taught only what other men have to say about the scriptures. They are instructed how to build and operate a church and establish all kinds of programs to encourage attendance, but the question of hearing the voice of God is often sadly neglected. A distorted sense of priority may become ingrained that dictates that a minister must periodically relocate to progressively larger and more prestigious churches in order to be "successful." Unfortunately, in order to survive in this kind of system, a clergyman often must learn to compromise. Instead of becoming God's leader and spokesman, he may become a "hireling," under obligation to teach only the accepted doctrines of his denomination. He must be careful not to offend people, particularly those with influence in his church. Excessive reference to holiness, commitment and God's judgment upon sin, for example, can make some people "uncomfortable." This can result in a reduction of donations or attendance, or even become a threat to job security.

When God establishes a local church in an area, He does so for a purpose. An unfortunate trend is the relocation of churches to the suburbs or other parts of the city whenever the neighborhood "changes." Instead of reaching out to the surrounding community, many churches become "ingrown." Then, as the racial or ethnic mix of the area begins to change, the members pack their bags and move elsewhere. Is this what God wants? I don't believe so. The Gospel of Jesus Christ is color-blind!

Persecution was the impetus that finally motivated the first-century Church at Jerusalem to begin spreading the Gospel outside of the city limits. The tendency of many churches is to become so closely knit that they become "cliques." Once we have been cleansed by the blood of Jesus Christ, there is a natural reluctance to go back into the world and reach out to the lost because it's an ugly, dirty, awful place. We would much prefer to remain in a spiritual greenhouse where we can grow under ideal circumstances. Souls are going to be saved in churches, but that is not the primary function of a church. The purpose of a church is to provide a place where believers can come together to worship and glorify God and to be encouraged, strengthened, and "refueled" before going back out into the world to share Christ. It is not a place to come to be isolated and entertained!

Within the true body of Christ, there are surely differences of opinion, as well as a remarkable diversity of personalities, backgrounds and lifestyles that are represented but where people are unified in Christ—i.e., the *truth*, these secondary considerations will only demonstrate the power of God to consolidate the hearts of people who might otherwise have little or nothing in common! Every structure of our physical bodies is intimately connected to those around it, and the body moves as a unit only as the brain provides direction. Within the body of Christ, the members are no less interrelated. In order for the Church to move as a coordinated unit, direction must come from one source: the head of the body, Jesus Christ:

> And He is the head of the Body, the Church: who is the Beginning, the Firstborn from the dead; that in all things He might have the preeminence. (Colossians 1:18)

> That there should be no schism in the Body; but that the members should have the same care for one another. And

whether one member suffer, all the members suffer with it; or one member be honoured, all the members rejoice with it. Now ye are the Body of Christ, and members in particular. (1 Corinthians 12:25–27)

In the course of our discussion, we have seen a fascinating correlation between the conception and gestation of a human being in its mother's womb, and the conversion and growth of the new believer in the body of Christ. Thus far, the parallel between the first birth and the second appears to be quite consistent and scriptural! Will we find this same consistency throughout the process of "pregnancy," including its final manifestation, the live birth? In the next section, we will closely examine this very intriguing question.

Part 3

The Live Birth: God's Promise Fulfilled

Congratulations! The momentous day has arrived. There is no aspect of universal human experience that elicits a greater sense of anticipation, joy, and excitement than the birth of a new baby! It is inspiring that—in our own culture at least—fathers are increasingly encouraged to observe and even participate in a miraculous event that was once the exclusive and jealously guarded domain of mothers, midwives and medical staffs!

We have discussed previously the integral role—which parallels that of the Holy Spirit in salvation—of the hormones in the process of conception and gestation; we can observe their continued involvement throughout labor and delivery as well. Hormonal activity stimulates the dilation of the cervix, providing passage for the baby. It is the release of oxytocin—the same hormone that enabled the sperm to reach the egg cell—that causes the uterine contractions. During labor, a woman's body experiences a myriad of complex and often bewildering hormonal changes, particularly during the phase known as *transition*. The degree of labor difficulty is guided by many variables, including medication, if any, administered to the mother. But when that newborn baby takes its first breath of air and begins to cry, mother's recollections of weeks of pregnancy discomfort and the more recent labor distress quickly fade!

> A woman when she is in travail hath sorrow, because her hour is come: but as soon as she is delivered of the child, she remembereth no more the anguish, for joy that a man is born into the world (John 16:21).

For the typical newborn, the transition from the familiar womb into the bright lights of a totally new environment is at once both dramatic and traumatic! Its senses are suddenly inundated by a deluge of amplified stimuli that bear only exaggerated resemblance to the sensations once filtered by its mother's protective body. Before, it had all of the *potential* of life outside of the womb. But now, having taken that initial breath, it *possesses* life! The *first* birth is now complete!

For the child of God, the transition from the "womb" of Christ into the kingdom of God is no less spectacular as he or she, attended by the Holy Spirit, passes through the *second* birth canal we know as *death*, or—for those who remain at the coming of Christ—the *Rapture*! Any trauma associated with the death experience will be instantaneously forgotten as we find ourselves at last set free from the confines of our corruptible flesh. Just as that new baby receives the breath of life, so those who are in Christ will receive the breath of *eternal* life!

> For we know that the whole Creation groaneth and travaileth in pain together until now. And not only they, but ourselves also, which have the first fruits of the Spirit, even we ourselves groan within ourselves, waiting for the adoption, to wit, the redemption of our body. (Romans 8:22–23)

> And if Christ be in you, the body is dead because of sin; but the Spirit is life because of righteousness. But if the Spirit of Him that raised up Jesus from the dead dwell in you, He that raised up Christ from the dead shall also quicken your mortal bodies by his spirit that dwelleth in you. (Romans 8:10–11)

No longer do we walk in the *promise* of eternal life; we now *possess* it! No longer do we cling to the *hope* of salvation; our salvation is *complete*! The birth of a new baby is "precious" to its parents; Psalm 116:15 says, "*Precious* in the sight of the Lord is the death of His saints." Like the anxious anticipation that attends the birth of a child, Creation itself eagerly awaits the revealing of God's own children on that day of redemption when the glorified saints—both dead and living—are caught up to be with the Lord!

> For I reckon that the sufferings of this present time are not worthy to be compared with the glory which shall be revealed in us. For the earnest expectation of the [Creation] waiteth for the manifestation of the sons of God. (Romans 8:18–19)

> So also is the resurrection of the dead. It is sown in corruption; it is raised in incorruption: it is sown in dishonour; it is raised in glory: it is sown in weakness; it is raised in power: it is sown a natural body; it is raised a spiritual body. There is a natural body, and there is a spiritual body. (2 Corinthians 15:42–44)

Scripturally, we are given a few glimpses of the glorious inheritance that lies on the "other side" for the children of God. Beyond these, however, there is only conjecture. One thing is certain: the change from this world to the next will be every bit as dramatic as that transformation experienced by the newborn baby!

> But as it is written, eye hath not seen, nor ear heard, neither have entered into the heart of man, the things which God hath prepared for them that love Him. (1 Corinthians 2:9)

> In My Father's house are many mansions: if it were not so, I would have told you. I go to prepare a place for you. And if I go to prepare a place for you, I will come again, and receive you unto Myself; that where I am, there ye may be also. (John 14:2–3)

In His Image

It should be the heart's desire of every born-again Christian to become as much like Jesus as possible. Psalm 17:15 says, "As for me, I will behold Thy face in righteousness: I shall be satisfied, when I awake, with *Thy likeness.*" Many believers who are not growing up into the fullness of Christ have the misconception that when they get to heaven they will be instantaneously transformed into the fully mature image of God's Son. That's the purpose of being *sealed* in Christ! Scripture indicates that there will be a hierarchy in the kingdom of heaven. There will be those called "great," but there will also be those considered the "least" (Matthew 5:19). Our reward will not be based upon what we have done for God, but rather, upon the extent to which we have yielded ourselves to the process of being molded into the image of His Son!

It is not long before family and friends begin to debate the question of a new baby's greater resemblance to one parent or the other. In some cases, it is obvious. When we consider the incarnation of Jesus Christ, we come to understand that He received half of his chromosomes from the *flesh*. The other half He received supernaturally from the *Holy Spirit*! Thus, within Jesus Christ was the genetic imprint of not only *man*, but also the *Word*. He was not only the *Son of Man;* He was also the *Son of God*. He was housed in a corruptible, fleshly tabernacle just as we are. He was faced with the choice—as we are—of yielding Himself to either the things of the Spirit or the things of the flesh. Jesus Christ chose to yield Himself to the Spirit just as He chose to yield His flesh to the Cross, "and being found in fashion as a man, He humbled Himself and became obedient unto death, even the death of the Cross" (Philippians 2:8). By doing so, He fulfilled the Law, was resurrected, and became the "Firstborn among many brethren" (Romans 8:29).

Many people wrongly assume that Jesus—because He was the Son of God— received a special "anointing" or power that prevented Him from sinning. If this had been the case, how could He possibly sympathize with the weakness of our flesh? Hebrews 4:15 says, "For we do not have a high priest who cannot sympathize with our weaknesses, but one who has been tempted in *all things* as we are, yet *without sin.*" The fact is Jesus Christ *chose* not to sin! That means Jesus never once compromised the will of His Father with regard to external human or satanic influences, or even to His own natural "human" perception, observation, or reasoning. Jesus's primary advantage over the rest of us was that His *Word* nature was already in place when He was born. We acquire ours when by faith we are born *again*! Yet Jesus still had to learn obedience "by the things which He suffered" in order to become the "author of eternal salvation unto all them that *obey* Him" (Hebrews 5:8–9). Jesus had the Law written upon His heart at the *first* birth; we receive it at the *second*! He was and will always be the only "begotten" Son of God, but He was the first of "*many* brethren." Because we have been "adopted" out of the world and "grafted" into Christ (Romans 11:24) does not make us any less the sons and daughters of God!

In our lost state, we are serving our flesh and sin. We have no choice in the matter. When we receive Christ, however, a spiritual conception takes place just as it did in the incarnation of Jesus Christ. When we receive the Word, our spirits—like the fertilized ovum—are made "alive." Within ourselves, we now have *two* natures. We can see this in Paul's reference to the battle being waged between the spirit and the flesh (Galatians 5:17). But now that we have the Word within us, we are no longer subject to the slavery of sin!

> Know ye not, that so many of us as were baptized into Jesus Christ were baptized unto His death? Therefore we are buried with Him by baptism into death: that like as Christ was raised up from the dead by the glory of the Father, even so we also should walk in newness of life. For if we have been planted together in the likeness of His death, we shall be also in the likeness of His resurrection: knowing this, that our old man is crucified with Him, that the body of sin might be destroyed, that hence-forth we should not serve sin. (Romans 6:3–6)

> But now being made free from sin, and become servants to God, ye have your fruit unto holiness, and the end everlasting life. (Romans 6:22)

In Christ, we are now free to choose, as Jesus was, whether to yield ourselves to the dictates of our flesh or to the Spirit of God. Our own spirits have been transformed, but our flesh must still be brought under subjection. In order to accomplish this, our minds must be "renewed" by the Word of God (Romans 12:2). This is an essential part of the process of growing up into Christ. Meanwhile, our flesh—which by its very nature continues to serve sin (Romans 7:25)—must *by faith* "go to the Cross" as we choose to die to our old way of life!

You have probably heard of *dominant* and *recessive* genes. Unlike the conceptus, you and I can choose—as Jesus did—to which "genetic tendency" we will yield ourselves. If we choose to feed ourselves the Word of God and obey it, the mind and the flesh will gradually be brought under subjection to the "dominant" Spirit, and we will begin to bear the *fruit of the Spirit* (Galatians 5:22–23). If we stubbornly continue to yield to our old nature, however, the flesh will become dominant and the Spirit "recessive"! The latter choice can carry with it, as we will see, serious consequences for the believer.

Understanding Salvation

Salvation, as we have seen, must be viewed as a *process* rather than merely as an isolated experience in the course of a human life. Peter wrote that we are "kept by the power of God *through faith unto salvation* ready to be *revealed* in the last time" (1 Peter 1:5). The source of much confusion is the predisposed view that conversion—i.e., the "salvation experience"—is a singular, instantaneous, and *irreversible* change in the eternal status of a human soul. This is only a partial truth; salvation is also *conditional*. The scriptures clearly illustrate this distinction:

> And that, knowing the time, that now it is high time to awake out of sleep: for now is our salvation nearer than when we believed. (Romans 13:11)

> For we are partakers of Christ *if* we hold the beginning of our confidence steadfast unto the end. (Hebrews 3:14, emphasis mine)

> But the one who endures to the end, it is he who shall be saved. (Matthew 24:13)

If the salvation experience of receiving Jesus Christ as Savior corresponds to conception—the beginning of the birth process—is it technically wrong to say that we were "born again" or "saved" at the moment we received Him? No! Why? How are we saved? "By grace through faith" (Ephesians 2:8). The scriptures tell us that we have been "born again" (1 Peter 1:23) and are "saved" (1 Corinthians 1:18) if we have received Christ. John writes that we "have" (present tense) eternal life if we have believed (1 John 5:13). If you or I were to die immediately upon receiving Christ, there is no question but that we would spend eternity in His presence. Our salvation would be assured; at the point of death, we would then *possess* our salvation.

At conversion, we receive the *promise* of God as Abraham did. Again, even though we are not "righteous," we receive the imputed righteousness of Christ based solely upon our faith in Him. A grasp of this principle is essential to a proper understanding of the doctrine of salvation. With respect to salvation, God is calling—as He did with Abraham—"those things which *be not as though they were*" (Romans 4:17). As long as we are alive and housed in a temporal, fleshly body, we have the "hope" (Titus 1:2) and the "promise" (1 John 2:25) of salvation by faith. We do not in actuality *possess* salvation—by its very definition—until God's *judgment* passes over us at our death, our resurrection, or by our being "caught up" and translated to be with Christ at His return. It is at that point God's promise is fulfilled, and we are quite literally born into the kingdom of God in a glorified body. Until that time, we are saved on the basis of our faith! The apostle Paul recognized this important principle.

> Well; because of unbelief they were broken off, and thou standest by faith. Be not highminded, but fear: For if God spared not the natural branches, take heed lest He also spare not thee. (Romans 11:20–21)

> Brethren, I count not myself to have apprehended [the resurrection from the dead] but this one thing I do, forgetting those things which are behind, and reaching forth unto those things which are before, I press toward the mark for the prize of the high calling of God in Christ Jesus. (Philippians 3:13–14)

As we have emphasized previously, until our salvation is actually revealed, we walk in the faith that our God is more than able to complete the process of the second birth!

> Being confident of this very thing, that He which hath begun a good work in you will perform it until the day of Jesus Christ. (Philippians 1:6)

When Jesus said, "Ye must be born again" (John 3:7), He was referring not only to the beginning of salvation but to the end of the process as well. If the evidence that I belong to Christ is present when I leave this world, there is absolutely no possibility that I could perish. For those who lack this evidence, there awaits only the terrible *second death* described in Revelation 20. If salvation is a process, how is it maintained? We have already seen that it is maintained the same way it is received: by *faith*!

> Blessed be the God and Father of our Lord Jesus Christ, which according to His abundant mercy hath begotten us again unto a lively hope by the resurrection of Jesus Christ from the dead, to an inheritance incorruptible, and reserved in Heaven for you who are kept by the power of God through faith unto salvation ready to be revealed in the last time. Wherein ye greatly rejoice, though now for a season, if need be, ye are in heaviness through manifold temptations: that the trial of your faith, being more precious than of gold that perisheth, though it be tried with fire, might be found unto praise and honor and glory at the appearing of Jesus Christ: whom having not seen, ye love; in whom, though now ye see Him not, yet believing, ye rejoice with joy unspeakable and full of glory: *receiving the end of your faith*, even *the salvation of your soul.* (1 Peter 3:3–9, emphasis mine)

Sealed in Christ

In the physical, the occurrence of conception does not inevitably insure a healthy, live birth. In addition to spontaneous natural abortions—as well as those induced artificially—there are a host of medical complications possible during gestation and even delivery that can result in the death of a conceptus. Parental genetic traits and a number of other factors—including drug or alcohol abuse, disease, and chemical or radiation exposure—can result in embryonic and fetal malformations that may or may not preclude a full-term pregnancy and a subsequent live birth.

We can see in the natural that it is possible for a conceptus to perish. Can we draw a parallel to the spiritual? We must exercise caution in doing so. Obviously, a believer's salvation is permanently assured when he or she goes to be with the Lord. What about those who are still physically alive and abiding in Christ? We distinctly find that, as long as we remain *in* Christ, there is nothing that can separate us from the presence of God.

> For I am persuaded, that neither death, nor life, nor angels, nor principalities, nor powers, nor things present, nor things to come, nor height, nor depth, nor any other creature, shall be able to separate us from the love of God, which is in Christ Jesus our Lord. (Romans 8:38–39)

> And I give unto them eternal life; and they shall never perish, neither shall any man pluck them out of My hand. (John 10:28)

Once we have been *sealed in Christ*, it should be obvious that there is absolutely no external force in heaven or on earth that can threaten the salvation process! Paul said in Romans 8:1 that there is "no condemnation for them which are *in* Christ Jesus." If this is the case, are there any *internal* factors that can cause a person who once received Christ to be "aborted" from the "womb" and thus no longer be *in* Christ? Is there anything within *me* that can destroy the lifeline of faith through which God maintains my salvation, resulting in spiritual *miscarriage*?

An interesting thing happens when a foreign object such as a marble is implanted in the uterus. For a period of two weeks or so, the symptoms of pregnancy will be present. When no evidence of growth is detected, however, the object will be sloughed off by the uterus. If an embryo dies following implantation, the usual production of hormones will cease and it will be similarly aborted.

Many professing Christians are taught never to question their salvation because that would be an expression of unbelief. This is contrary to scripture. Paul admonished the Corinthian Christians to "examine" themselves to see if they remained "in the faith" (2 Corinthians 13:5). Proverbs 28:26 suggests that a man whose life is dictated by his own heart is a "fool." If my own heart tells me that I'm right with God, but my actions, words, and attitudes continue to indicate otherwise, then I have every reason to examine my salvation! Without question, the best indicator of my walk with God is not what I say or what my heart tells me, but the *fruit* being manifested in my life.

> Now the works of the flesh are manifest, which are these; adultery, fornication, uncleanness, lasciviousness, idolatry, witchcraft, hatred, variance, emulations, wrath, strife, seditions, heresies, envyings, murders, drunkenness, revelings, and such like: of the which I tell you before, as I have also told you in time past, that they which do such things shall not inherit the kingdom of God. But the fruit of the Spirit is love, joy, peace, longsuffering, gentleness, goodness, faith, meekness, temperance: against such there is no law. And they that are Christ's have crucified the flesh with the affections and lusts. (Galatians 5:19–24)

Recall the incident in which Jesus cursed the fig tree (Matthew 21:19). This was obviously done as an object lesson to the disciples. Why did Jesus curse the tree? Because of the absence of fruit! The same test applies to you and me. If I am walking in obedience to God's Word and my faith remains intact, my life will inevitably begin to manifest the fruit of the Spirit, the "peaceable fruit of *righteousness*" (Hebrews 12:11). What will eventually happen to the "born-again- by-faith" believer who has been grafted into the Vine of Christ, but who ceases to abide in Him and bear fruit unto God? Jesus Himself answers this very question:

> Abide in Me, and I in you. As the branch cannot bear fruit of itself, except it abide in the vine; no more can ye, except ye abide in Me. I am the Vine, ye are the branches: he that abideth in Me, and I in him, the same bringeth forth much fruit: for without Me ye can do nothing. If a man abide not in Me, he is cast forth as a branch, and is withered; and men gather them, and cast them into the fire, and they are burned. (John 15:4–6)

As the parable of the sower in chapter 13 of Matthew illustrates, there are those who initially receive the Word with "joy," but because of tribulation, persecution, the cares of the world or the deceitfulness of riches, they at some point cease to abide and grow in Christ and consequently abandon their faith. The Bible explicitly says that those who endure until the *end* are going to be saved. It does not promise salvation to those who merely begin a walk with God. We can begin to see the significance of Jesus's warning to His disciples not to fear those capable of destroying the flesh, but rather, to fear God, who is "able to destroy both soul and body in hell" (Matthew 10:28). We can also see the serious implication of Paul's admonition not to grieve the Holy Spirit by whom we are sealed in Christ. It is no great matter for the hormones to direct the removal of the cervical plug and stimulate contractions to abort a dead fetus from the womb! Similarly, a believer who has "died on the vine" will eventually be rejected by the Holy Spirit from the protective spiritual "womb" of Jesus Christ.

Whenever we cease to grow in Christ, we become "lukewarm." I will drink an occasional cup of hot tea, and I love iced tea, but there's something almost nauseating about *lukewarm* tea. God feels the same way about the Church; He will eventually "vomit" out those believers who have allowed their hearts to be hardened and have permitted their love and zeal for Him to be compromised. We tend to forget that the letter to Laodicea in Revelation 3 is written to people in the Church, not to people in the world! For our generation, it is a compassionate last day's warning and a call to repentance for those whose faith has dried up and whose salvation is jeopardized because of sin, pride, and compromise.

> I know thy works, that thou are neither cold nor hot: I would that thou wert cold or hot, so then because thou art lukewarm, and neither cold nor hot, I will [vomit] thee out of My mouth. Because thou sayest, "I am rich, and increased with goods, and have need of nothing," and knowest not that thou art wretched, and miserable, and poor, and blind, and naked: I counsel thee to buy of Me gold tried in the fire, that thou mayest be rich; and white raiment, that thou mayest be clothed, and that the shame of thy nakedness do not appear;

and anoint thine eyes with eye salve, that thou mayest see. (Revelation 3:15–18)

In spiritual context, when a person is finally "vomited" out of God's mouth, they are *outside* of Christ. Once in this condition, they no longer wear the "white raiment" which is the *righteousness of Christ;* they have compromised the "gold tried in the fire," the precious *faith* that God desires to refine through the salvation process. They are spiritually *blind*. Even so, God has not given up on them! In the verses that follow, the mercy and long-suffering nature of God are manifested:

As many as I love, I rebuke and chasten: be zealous therefore, and repent. Behold, I stand at the door and knock: if any man hear My voice, and open the door, I will come into him, and will sup with him, and he with Me. (Revelation 3:19–20)

Notice that, even in their desperate state, they have not been completely cut off from the love of God. He will even send chastisement to try to bring them to their senses. Even though Jesus Christ is now outside, for a period of time He continues to knock on the door of their hearts, trying to reestablish His rightful place in their lives. Like the vinedresser in the parable of the unfruitful fig tree in Luke 13, Jesus wants to give them another opportunity to repent and begin to bear fruit unto God. He is waiting with open arms to restore every broken penitent to the household of heaven!

The parable of the prodigal son is much more readily applicable to those who were once abiding members of the family of God than to those who have never known Him at all. As the father joyfully said of the younger son who had squandered his inheritance:

For this son of mine was *dead*, and is *alive* again; he was lost and is found. And they began to be merry. (Luke 15:24)

If repentance is forthcoming, God will do a miraculous thing! Throughout history, He has often superseded the natural by doing things that are impossible from the perspective of human understanding. The miracle of the Virgin Birth and the resurrection of Lazarus's dead body from the grave are just two of many examples. Under normal circumstances, once a conceptus is aborted there is nothing that can be done to save it. God in His mercy, however, is able to supernaturally "reimplant" that aborted soul into Christ; He can "regraft" that severed "branch" and restore the salvation process (Romans 11:23). A "tare" can become "wheat"! Another example of God's ability to transcend the natural is that a newly fertilized ovum is not viable; it is not able to survive on its own. Yet a person who dies immediately upon receiving Christ—like the thief on the Cross—will spend eternity in God's presence! His newly activated faith, though immature, is intact and uncontaminated by *unbelief.*

Faith and Works

As God is establishing "line upon line" and "precept upon precept" in our hearts through His Word, we must be careful that we do not isolate a particular scripture and build a doctrine upon it without consideration for its context in the entirety of God's Word. For example, Ephesians 2:8–9 says, "For by grace are ye saved through faith; and that not of yourselves: it is the gift of God: not of works, lest any man should boast." Clearly, an entire lifetime of my own "good deeds" can do absolutely nothing to cause me to merit God's free gift of salvation. Does this mean, however, that "works" (i.e., *acting* upon faith) have nothing to do with salvation? God forbid! Consider James 2:14–26:

> What doth it profit, my brethren, though a man say he hath faith, and have not works? Can faith [alone] save him? If a brother or sister be naked, and destitute of daily food and one of you say unto them, "Depart in peace, be ye warmed and filled"; notwithstanding ye give them not those things which are needful to the body; what doth it profit? Even so, faith, if it hath not works, is dead, being alone. Yea, a man may say, "Thou hast faith, and I have works: show me thy faith without thy works, and I will shew thee my faith by my works." Thou believest that there is one God; thou doest well: the devils also believe, and tremble. But wilt thou know, O vain man, that faith without works is dead? Was not Abraham our father justified by works, when he had offered Isaac his son upon the altar? Seest thou how faith wrought

with his works, and by works was faith made perfect? And the scripture was fulfilled which saith, "Abraham believed God, and it was imputed unto him for righteousness": and he was called the Friend of God. Ye see then how by works a man is justified, and not by faith only. Likewise also was not Rahab the harlot justified by works, when she had received the messengers, and had sent them out another way? For as the body without the spirit is dead, so faith without works is dead also.

If my doctrine says that a mental or even a verbal acknowledgement of Jesus Christ is the sole requisite for beginning and maintaining the salvation process, then by implication the demons of hell are candidates for redemption! Faith, untested and untried, is worthless. James likens faith without works to a dead body without a spirit! What, then, is God's definition of "works"? What are the works that are inextricably tied to faith? Jesus made the statement: "This is the work of God, that ye *believe* on Him whom He hath sent" (John 6:29). How is the *act* of believing distinguished from *faith* itself? Believing, the "works" of God, is also the *exercise* of our faith; it is applying *obedience* to that faith! As James carefully explains, the great men and women of faith in the scriptures were justified only when they chose, by an act of their will, to put actions to the faith God had given them! Interestingly, Moses was rebuked for his unbelief when he angrily struck the Rock in the wilderness contrary to God's directive (Numbers 20:12).

When a person has been drawn by God, the very act of surrendering their will to the unconditional lordship of Jesus Christ is a beautiful example of works (confessing) and faith (believing) operating together!

> But what saith it? The Word is nigh thee, even in thy mouth, and in thy heart: that is, the Word of faith, which we preach; that if thou shalt *confess with thy mouth* the Lord Jesus, and shalt *believe in thine heart* that God hath raised Him from the dead, thou shalt be saved. For with the heart man believeth unto righteousness; and with the mouth confession is made unto salvation (Romans 10:8–10).

Unless I understand God's definition of what it means to *confess* Jesus as Lord, I may be tempted to build a doctrine on scriptures like John 3:16: "For God so loved the world, that He gave His only begotten Son, that whosoever believeth in Him should not perish, but have everlasting life." This beautiful truth of God's Word finds its proper context in other scriptures such as one we have quoted previously: "Though He were a Son, yet learned He obedience by the things which He suffered; and being made perfect, He became the author of eternal salvation unto *all that obey Him*" (Hebrews 5:8–9). Most people equate "works" with "good deeds," but man's concept of works has nothing to do with salvation. It should be apparent that having God's *faith* is worthless unless God's *works* are applied! Jesus never spoke any words or performed any actions unless His Father first granted the faith to do so. If Jesus Christ had not applied works to God's faith, He would not have gone to the Cross and our redemption would not have been purchased.

The Enemy of Faith

What will happen to my faith if I fail to apply God's works (i.e., *obedience*) to it? As we have seen, "faith without works is dead." There is only one thing that can cause a born-again-by-faith believer to abort his or her salvation, and that is for their faith to *die*. The mortal enemy of faith is better known in scripture, not as the failure to apply obedience to faith, but as *unbelief*. Previously, we mentioned that souls perish ultimately because of unbelief; this can apply to a believer as well as to a nonbeliever. Conspicuously missing from those things in scripture that "cannot separate us" from the love of God are rebellion and unbelief.

Unbelief declares, "I don't really *believe* that God is going to judge my sin. After all, I'm a child of the King. Besides, I'm not really bad enough to go to hell." Unbelief says, "I refuse to spend time alone with God and in the meditation of His Word because I don't really *believe* that God requires it or that He is a 'rewarder of them that diligently seek Him'" (Hebrews 11:6). Unbelief proclaims, "I don't really *believe* He's serious when God says I won't see His face without holiness. Besides, I've given Him every opportunity to make me like Jesus and all I do is struggle with sin. I'm just going to go on doing my own thing." If I continue in unbelief, my faith will eventually die, and I will cease to be a *believer*! Unless I repent, I will then—as much of Israel did for the same reason—perish in a spiritual wilderness without ever experiencing an intimate walk with God or knowing the joy and the peace of entering into God's promised land of "rest."

> Take heed, brethren, lest there be in any of you an evil heart of unbelief, in departing from the living God. But exhort one another daily, while it is called today; lest any of you be hardened through the deceitfulness of sin. For we are made partakers of Christ, *if* we hold the beginning of our confidence steadfast unto the end. (Hebrews 3:12–14)

> There remaineth therefore a rest to the people of God. For he that is entered into His rest, he also hath ceased from his own works, as God did from His. Let us labour therefore to enter into that rest, lest any man fall after the same example of unbelief. (Hebrews 4:9–11)

If we continue to resist the efforts of the Holy Spirit to bring conviction of— and deliverance from—the sins of our flesh, that resistance becomes *sin*, which is *rebellion* against God. Rebellion is more than just disobedience; in reality, it is the manifestation of unbelief. It is this unbelief that will destroy our faith. The scripture says that we have "not yet resisted unto blood, striving against sin" (Hebrews 12:4). We are also told, "he that hath suffered in the flesh hath ceased from sin" (1 Peter 4:1). Just as God promised Israel that He would enable them to conquer the nations representing sin, so He has promised us the ability to overcome the sin strongholds in our lives through Jesus Christ.

> But the God of all grace, who hath called us unto His eternal glory by Jesus Christ, after that ye have suffered a while, make you perfect, establish, strengthen, settle you. (1 Peter 5:10)

Contrary to what many people are taught, there will not be any "carnal" Christians found in the kingdom of heaven. Unrepentant persons who habitually practice sin including theft, alcohol abuse, greed, hateful speech and sexual immorality (1 Corinthians 6:9–10) have chosen a path that will finally result in the abortion of any hope of salvation. Jesus indicated that the attitude of the heart and the commission of the actual sin are no different in God's sight (Matthew 5:28). Hebrews 12:14 says, "Pursue peace with all men, and holiness, without which no man shall see the Lord." To believe that God is suddenly going to replace the deeds of our flesh with the fruit of His righteousness when we die is a false hope and reflects a serious lack of understanding of God's Word! If anything, God's requirement of holiness under the New Covenant is *greater* than under the Old. How will God perceive those who pass from this life to the next without the clear "genetic" imprint of Jesus Christ upon their hearts?

As a dream when one awaketh; so, O Lord, when Thou awakest, *Thou shalt despise their image* (Psalm 73:20).

It should be quite evident that the only potential threat to our salvation does not originate from God, nor from any other force in the universe, but from within *ourselves*! It comes back to our free will and whether we choose to yield to God's Spirit or to the desires of our own flesh. To continue to yield to my old nature is to continue in sin and unbelief. The destruction of my faith will be reflected by the absence of the fruit of righteousness. And, as we have seen, the presence of *fruit* will ultimately be a test of our salvation.

Jesus's parable of the talents in Matthew 25 is not merely a lesson on being a good steward of God's resources. More importantly, it is a parable of *faith*. God gives every person a different measure of faith, but always enough faith to believe the Gospel and receive Jesus Christ as Savior. If, however, that person does not act upon that faith, it will be taken away. As long as the evidence of faith is present, there is no person on earth who is a candidate for hell, but this same faith, as well as the Word that causes it to be activated, will ultimately be revoked from the hearts of those who reject God or those who give themselves over to apostasy.

For he that hath, to him shall be given: and he that hath not, from him shall be taken even that which he hath. (Mark 4:25)

What is our part as believers in maintaining that precious *gold*, the gift of faith through which God, in turn, maintains our salvation?

"So then faith cometh by hearing, and hearing by the Word of God" (Romans 10:17). Faith is maintained the same way it is activated: by the *Word of God*. Our faith lives and grows as we feed ourselves with the Word of God! Have you ever noticed how difficult it becomes to trust God when you are entertaining sin in your life? The last thing in the world you want to do in this state is to pray, read your Bible, go to church, or be around joyful Christians.

A good illustration of what sin can do to the spirit may be found in the context of dental hygiene. In both humans and animals, a tooth that is not cared for can accumulate tartar below the gum line, resulting in erosion of the tooth enamel and finally producing an abscess. This abscess, in turn, can release a strain of streptococcal bacteria into the bloodstream. These bacteria can attach themselves to heart valves causing serious illness and eventually, death. At first, it seems hard to believe that neglecting a tooth could result in the death of the entire body, but the same principle holds true spiritually if we refuse to deal with sin in our lives!

What is the key to overcoming sin? It is not saying "No!" to sin, but saying "Yes!" to God! As we have seen, *true* believing is accompanied by the "works" of God: the *exercise* of our faith; it is abiding in Christ! The only way to abide in Christ is to walk in obedience to God's commandments, spending time alone with Him and meditating daily upon His Word. As we seek God with all of our hearts, His Word gradually becomes a part of us and we can begin to know Him. Our minds and thoughts are renewed, and we will begin to see, through the trials and "pruning" of our faith, the fruit of righteousness in our lives.

It will not happen instantaneously! We have seen that salvation is not just a matter of believing "once"; it is based on a continuous *walk* of faith. This is why the scripture speaks of our need of endurance. James writes, "But be ye *doers* of the Word, and not *hearers* only, deceiving your own selves" (James 1:22). As we continue to abide in Christ, we will discover a growing ability to walk in obedience to God's Word and to overcome sin in our lives. This is all part of the process of growing up into Christ!

Counting the Cost

In the course of our study, we have seen that the salvation of a human soul— the process we know as the second birth—is not merely a matter of spiritual conception. Nor does it consist of conception and gestation alone. Salvation finds its culmination in the final phase of the process, which is a live birth into the kingdom of God.

When a new baby leaves the hospital, it is generally assumed that a loving, supportive family unit is waiting with open arms to welcome and nurture the new arrival in a warm, totally protected environment. In practical reality, we know that this—sadly—is not always the case. What about that immature believer, whose newly conceived spirit must be ushered into the incubative structure we know as the *Church*? Can we rest assured that the Church—God's pragmatic representation of the body of Christ—is always a safe haven for the collective growth and development of new Christians?

Unfortunately, we are surrounded today by a profusion of "cheap" gospels which have little or nothing to do with the Cross of Jesus Christ. There is, in fact, a false conversion, a terrifying and satanic *counterfeit conception* that can occur when unprepared hearts embrace the religious doctrines and teachings of men instead of the Word of God, as the Pharisees did. That is another topic. But whether it is an unbalanced proclamation of worldly prosperity and success in this life or a message of salvation without repentance, any gospel that costs me nothing is—to use Paul's term—"another" gospel (Galatians 1:6).

Jesus said, "I am the *way*, the *truth*, and the *life*: no man cometh unto the Father, but by me" (John 14:6). The path to resurrection and glorification for not only the "Firstborn," but for the rest of God's children as well, must lead first to the Cross! The apostle Paul said, "For the preaching of the Cross is to them that perish foolishness; but unto us which are saved it is the power of God" (1 Corinthians 1:18). The Cross is a picture of *death*! What died on the Cross? Sinful flesh! It symbolizes the death sentence we receive in our flesh when we choose to follow Jesus Christ in obedience to His Word. There is no resurrection—there is no live birth—except through the Cross!

> And whosoever doth not bear his cross, and come after Me, cannot be my disciple. For which of you, intending to build a tower, sitteth not down first, and counteth the cost, whether he have sufficient to finish it? Lest haply, after he hath laid the foundation, and is not able to finish it, all that behold it begin to mock him, saying, "This man began to build, and was not able to finish." Or what king, going to make war against another king, sitteth not down first, and consulteth whether he be able with ten thousand to meet him that cometh against him with twenty thousand? Or else, while the other is yet a great way off, he sendeth ambassage, and desireth conditions of peace. So likewise, whosoever he be of you that forsaketh not all that he hath, he cannot be My disciple. (Luke 14:27–33)

The scriptures tell us that it is far better to never begin a walk with God than to make that commitment and then fall away. Jesus said, "No man, having put his hand to the plough, and looking back, is fit for the kingdom of God" (Luke 9:62). Peter warns against the false teachers and purveyors of cheap gospels who introduce "damnable heresies" and entice others to ignore the true cost of following Christ.

> For when they speak great swelling words of vanity, they allure through the lusts of the flesh, through much wantonness, those that were [barely] escaped from them who live in error. While they promise them liberty, they themselves are the servants of corruption: for of whom a man is overcome, of the same is he brought in bondage. For if after they have escaped the pollutions of the world through the knowledge of the Lord and Savior Christ, they are again entangled therein, and overcome, the latter end is worse with them than the beginning. For it had been better for them not to have known the way of righteousness, than, after they have known it, to turn from the holy commandment delivered unto them. (2 Peter 2:18–21)

The Son of God is not returning for a carnal Church that is fraught with internal strife, compromise, "fallen" ministers and priests, false doctrine, and controversy. Rather, He is returning for the remnant of those who—like the wise virgins in Jesus's parable—have prepared their hearts for His arrival. He is coming, with great anticipation, to redeem His Father's sons and daughters who, collectively, constitute His own *bride*; a bride without "spot," "wrinkle" or "blemish" (Ephesians 5:27). We must recognize that when Christ returns, He will come not only as a redeemer but also as a righteous *judge*. The awesome, glorified Christ seen by John on Patmos was quite different from the person he had known and loved years before. Not only will there be God's terrible great white throne judgment and the second death for those who perish, but those who experience the second birth must also stand before the judgment seat of Christ and give an account of their stewardship.

Christians do a terrible injustice to the unsaved when they discourage them from counting the cost of a walk with God. Many people will come—as they did after Jesus fed the multitudes—for what they can get from God, but when the Word begins to make demands of *change* upon their lives, they quickly fall away. A young lady who was an alcoholic came to me for counseling, but I soon realized after a few sessions that I wasn't helping her. I told her that if she wanted help, she would have to start reading her Bible and going to a church where the Word was preached. I told her not to call me again unless she was in compliance. She called me a few months later in a state of drunken depression, looking for a sympathetic ear. "Have you been reading your Bible and going to church?" I inquired. "No." I said goodbye and hung up on her. The same scenario occurred again on several occasions and each time I would give the same response. Finally, she stopped calling. Three years later, she called again. "I wanted to let you know that I finally came to the conclusion that I was dying. I decided that I might as well die in church as outside of it, so I started attending, and I've gotten saved! I wanted to thank you because it never would have happened if you had let me cry on your shoulder!"

People do not get genuinely saved until they come to the spiritual understanding that they have been tried before God's court, found guilty according to the Law, and condemned to death. It is only then that they can recognize their only possible recourse: to cry out to their Judge for *mercy*! It is at that point hope appears as Jesus Christ calls them forth out of their spiritual graves: "The hour is coming, and *now is*, when the *dead* shall hear the voice of the Son of God, and they that hear shall *live!*" (John 5:25).

If someone is not willing to seek God for themselves, the worst thing a believer can do is to offer them a cheap gospel that makes no demands of change upon them. The tendency in the Church today is to try to make it "easy" for people to come to Christ. The apostle Paul was not saved on the road to Damascus where he encountered Jesus Christ. He was not saved until God directed him to Ananias and showed him all of the things he would have to suffer for the sake of the Gospel (Acts 9:16). It was only then that Paul called on the name of the Lord and received the baptism of repentance. John the Baptist, in the power of the Holy Spirit, prepared the way for Jesus Christ by preaching the baptism of repentance from sins. The pattern is still the same. Repentance *always* precedes salvation. There can be no salvation without repentance! If we are not willing to turn from our sin, we have not repented.

For this stubborn flesh to surrender control to the unconditional authority of Jesus Christ inevitably presents, at some level, a *crisis*. It is often said with great evangelical fervor, "Jesus doesn't clean His fish *before* He catches them!" More accurately, Jesus doesn't catch His fish until they *come clean*. Unless God reveals it, you and I have no way of knowing what issues may need to be addressed in a person's life before faith can be activated in their hearts.

Years ago, while ministering on a parking lot for a period of time, our church group would encounter "Christians" who had cigarettes in their mouths, a beer can in one hand and Bible in the other. They proclaimed a "salvation" based on a "sinner's prayer" that would allow a person to "receive Christ," yet continue to live like the world. Many people are eager to purchase this kind of inexpensive insurance policy, but it is going to be consumed by hell's inferno alongside the policy holder. A person is not going to be saved unless he or she has been drawn by God and is willing to repent. When people are told the truth, there is a much greater chance that they will, in turn, respond honestly and acknowledge the fact that they are not ready to pay the price of dying to themselves. Instead of going away thinking they are "saved," they know they have the freedom to come back if and when they *are* ready!

A young woman was invited to one of our Sunday services and was singing along with the congregation. When she got to a well-known hymn that begins with the lyrics, "*I'd rather have Jesus than silver or gold,*" she stopped, turned to the member who had invited her and said, "I can't sing that!" She wasn't ready to meet Jesus at that point, but at least she was being *honest*.

The message of the Cross is not, nor has it ever been, "popular." There is much false teaching today that denies the judgment of God upon sin and attributes suffering among Christians to a "lack of faith." Yet God's Word says that we are "joint heirs with Christ; if so be that we suffer with Him" (Romans 8:17). We are living in an age in which much of the Church has grown lukewarm, repentance is no longer preached, and sin is no longer challenged. The scripture says, "The fear of the Lord is to hate evil" (Proverbs 8:13). If we do not *hate sin*, we do not *fear God*! We live in the midst of an entire generation—both in and outside of the Church—that does not fear God or really believe in His coming judgment. Consequently, many people have no compunction about picking and choosing those parts of God's Word they are willing to accept or obey while discarding the rest. This is unbelief and it will eventually destroy their faith!

Whenever we choose to reject a single portion of God's Word, we have fallen into a pattern of unbelief. When God's Word says that we must *forgive*, for example, many people hold on to their grudges or bitterness because, "I'm *justified*." What they are saying is, "God's Word doesn't apply to *me*," or "*my* situation is *different*." God has granted us time in *this* life to be reconciled to Himself and to those around us. It is while we are in the "womb" of Christ that we are given the opportunity to grow up into the image of God's Son!

There is not one of us who enjoys suffering, but the act of resisting sin is often quite painful to flesh that is used to having its own way! The cost to be counted is far greater, however, if we choose to yield to our carnal nature than if we yield our flesh—with God's help—to the death of the Cross. The Word of God declares that what we sow we will also reap (Galatians 6:7). Anyone who is being honest will acknowledge that sin can be quite pleasurable for a period of time, but only until we begin to reap the consequences of it.

When I share with people, I often point out the fact that if there were only one chance in one billion that the Word of God is true and that hell is a reality, that is still too great a risk not to search out the truth with all diligence. What is the benefit of a few moments or even a few years of pleasure upon this earth if I am forever tormented in such a place? What is the significance of seventy or so years upon this earth against the scope of eternity? Only a fool would sell out so cheaply. Yet untold billions of souls will make this choice.

There is much reference in Christian circles today to a great last days harvest of souls and a worldwide "revival." But what does the scripture say will precede the return of Jesus Christ?

> And then shall many be offended, and shall betray one another, and shall hate one another. And many false prophets shall rise, and shall deceive many. And because iniquity shall abound, the love of many will wax cold. (Matthew 24:12)

God's Word tells us that men will grow increasingly wicked as time grows short. Jesus said that the final days would be just as they were in the days of Noah (Matthew 24:37). Noah was a preacher of righteousness for over a hundred years and did not see a single convert outside of his own household. In every generation, only a remnant is going to be saved. But Jesus is not coming to judge the earth as long as there remains a single lost person who is seeking God with all of his heart!

Revival, if it is to occur, must take place, not in the world, but in the hearts of God's people! The biggest hindrance to God's harvest is not the sin in the world, but the sin in the *Church*.

> If My people, which are called by My name, shall humble themselves, and pray, and seek My face, and turn from their wicked ways; then will I hear from Heaven, and will forgive their sin and will heal their land. (2 Chronicles 7:14)

The primary reason we don't see God's healing is because of lukewarm, uncommitted, sinning Christians who don't look like Jesus

Christ! Why should the lost come to Christ when they don't see any difference between themselves and those who go to church on the weekend to have someone make them "feel good"? A day hardly goes by without press coverage of "militant" Christians breaking the laws of the land or a sex scandal in the "Church." Except for a small remnant here and there, God's people have ceased to be the "light" and the "salt" that God ordained them to be (Matthew 5:13–16).

God's impending judgment will begin in the Church. The spiritual counterfeits, or "tares" will be gathered out and burned prior to the harvest of the righteous "wheat" (Matthew 13:40–43). How much better it will be for the ones who yield in obedience to God now than for those who wait until it is too late! There are still many souls who can be reached for the kingdom of God, but until Christians decide to pray, come out of the world and be a "separate" people, the harvest yield will fall far short of its potential.

Mass evangelism is not God's plan for building the Church. Jesus preached to the masses on occasion, but He spent most of His time with a few committed men, poured Himself into them, and then told them to follow His example. The problem with most mass evangelism is the absence of any effective follow-up. Many who are involved in such ministries have not counted the cost of discipling those new believers. Even when a convert is referred to a local church, there is not always a guarantee that a particular church will provide a safe and scriptural nursery environment for the new "babe" in Christ. In short, the survival rate of converts through mass evangelism—even by the admission of some ministries—is abysmally low.

When a new baby is born, the parents don't leave it behind and return for it in eighteen years! If a new baby is not fed, it will soon die. Within a few weeks after a mass evangelism campaign, many of the "babes" are spiritually dead: from starvation due to a lack of the Word and exposure to the elements of Satan's deception. Every one of us is born a spiritual babe in Christ. When a new baby is born physically, it must be cleaned up and cared for. If extrinsic birth fluids and tissues are not removed, bacterial ulcers can form which may result in death. When a person receives Christ, there is a period of nurturing and discipleship which is a critical part of growing up into the image of Jesus Christ. When a soul is born by faith into the kingdom of God, he or she must be gathered into the arms of the Church; this is God's way of providing a covering and protection for them, especially until the basic doctrines of Christ can be established in their lives. A new spiritual babe in Christ that is abandoned after birth probably has little more hope of survival on its own than its physical counterpart. As we have seen, it is better not to come to Christ than to come and then fall away. There is little point in sowing seed in a field if it is not going to be watered and cultivated. As we have indicated, unless we recognize this principle, we may become poor laborers in God's harvest. We may stand before the Lord of the Harvest only to find that the fruit of much of our labors has long ago perished in the field!

Before we choose to begin a walk with God, or encourage someone else to do the same, we must—in all fairness to ourselves and others—consider the cost involved in such a commitment. For many, it may result in losing friends or alienating loved ones. For others, choosing this path will require giving up precious idols in their lives. For some, a walk with God will—as in Paul's case— mandate great suffering and persecution. For every follower of Jesus Christ, one price tag will be the same: dying to *self* as we follow in obedience the steps of Jesus Christ leading to the Cross!

Marriage Made in Heaven

Our previous study of the reproductive process as it illustrates salvation would be incomplete without at least some mention of its proper context—that is, the marriage relationship between a man and a woman. The following quotation is taken from the Good News translation of the Bible:

> For you know the instructions we gave you, by the authority of the Lord Jesus. This is God's will for you: He wants you to be holy and completely free from immorality. Each of you men should know how to take a wife in a holy and honorable way not with a lustful desire, like the heathen who do not know God. In this matter, then, no man should do wrong to his brother or violate his rights. We have told

you this before, we strongly warned you, that the Lord will punish those who do such wrongs. (1 Thessalonians 4:2–6)

It is true that God created mankind with a sexual desire, but when this desire is controlled by the flesh, it becomes *lust*. Lust, in turn, conceives *sin*, which results in *death* (James 1:15). When directed by the spirit, however, this God- given instinct becomes an instrument of God's *agape* love, which is unselfish giving without a demand of reciprocation! Only when a man and woman become one in the spirit *and* in the flesh can love find its ultimate fulfillment in the context of a holy marriage covenant! Jesus alluded to the deep spiritual significance of this institution in the following passage:

> And He answered and said, "Have you not read, that He who created them from the beginning made them male and female, and said, 'For this cause a man shall leave his father and mother, and shall cleave to his wife; and the two shall become one flesh?' Consequently they are no more two, but one flesh. What therefore God has joined together, let no man separate." (Matthew 19:4–6)

Marriage was designed by God to give mankind a physical picture of the kind of intimate, holy, and pure spiritual relationship He desires to have with every born-again believer. The apostle Paul speaks of the fact that in marriage is contained the "mystery" of Christ and the Church. In fact, the metaphorical use of engagement and marriage to illustrate salvation is thematic in the scriptures.

> For I am jealous for you with a Godly jealously; for I betrothed you to one husband, that to Christ I might present you as a pure virgin. (2 Corinthians 11:2)

> Husbands, love your wives, just as Christ also loved the Church and gave Himself up for her; that He might-sanctify her, having cleansed her by the washing of water with the Word, that He might present to Himself the Church in all her glory, having no spot or wrinkle or any such thing; but that she should be holy and blameless. So husbands ought also to love their own wives as their own bodies. He who loves

his own wife loves himself; for no one ever hated his own flesh, but nourishes and cherishes it, just as Christ also does the Church, because we are members of His body, of His flesh, and of His bones. For this cause shall man leave his father and mother, and shall be joined unto his wife, and they two shall be one flesh. This is a great mystery: but I speak concerning Christ and the church. Nevertheless let every one of you in particular so love his wife even as himself; and the wife see that she reverenceher husband. (Ephesians 5:25–33)

It is noteworthy that throughout the Bible, God likens spiritual apostasy and rebellion to fornication and adultery. The image of Jesus as the bridegroom and the Church as the bride reflect the sanctity and holiness of marriage as God intended it to be. The degree of fulfillment in a person's marriage is perhaps one of the best barometers of their walk with God. Marriage, then, not only provides us with proper context of physical procreation and family, but it also gives us a beautiful picture of the spiritual union between man and God through the person of Jesus Christ. It is this spiritual union that becomes the basis for the Church, God's instrument for the reproduction of souls to be born into the kingdom of God!

At Home with God

For me and for many people, *home* has some very special connotations. Home is a place where I can just be myself. Home is comfortable. Home is a refuge where someone is waiting and always glad to see me when I arrive. Home is where I feel that I belong even when few, if any, words are spoken. It was the thought of home that motivated the prodigal son to return to his loving father. Being alone in God's presence should be a foretaste of what my eternal home will be like. God doesn't look forward to a lot of unnecessary conversation and endless petitions on my part. He's just glad to see me! He just wants us to come home.

I recall the times that I got in trouble at school as a youngster. In those instances, the prospect of going home brought fear instead of eager anticipation. Until we turn from them, our sins cause a similar rift in our relationship with God. Where there is unconfessed sin, the desire to be at home with God is quickly diminished. As believers, we must recognize that God is a heavenly Father with immeasurable love and compassion for His children, but He is also a God of judgment. He hates sin! But as long as we are sealed and hidden in Christ and continue to yield ourselves in obedience to the Word and to the purification of our faith, we remain under *grace*. We are covered by the blood of Jesus Christ and do not need to fear God's judgment. Again, the key to a successful Christian walk is not saying "No!" to sin but "Yes!" to God. There is no victory in rigid adherence to a negative list of "Thou shalt not's!" Instead, the overcoming believer learns to obey God's *positive* admonitions.

> And Thou shalt love the Lord thy God with all thy heart, and with all thy soul, and with all thy mind, and with all thy strength: this is the first commandment. (Mark 12:30)

> This book of the Law shall not depart out of thy mouth; but Thou shalt meditate therein day and night, that thou mayest observe to do according to all that is written therein: for then thou shalt make thy way prosperous, and then thou shalt have good success. (Joshua 1:8)

Expectant parents are often heard saying, "I don't care if it's a boy or a girl. I just want it to be *healthy*." More than we can possibly imagine, our heavenly Father wants to see His children grow up into the image of Jesus Christ and experience a healthy, live birth—an "abundant entrance"—into the kingdom of God! Jesus said, "Fear not, little flock; for it is your Father's good pleasure to give you the kingdom" (Luke 12:32).

For the moment, I am housed in corruptible flesh and am born again on the basis of God's promise by *faith*. But one day, faith will have accomplished its purpose and I will enjoy the literal transformation of birth from this life to the next and will know the eternal reality of being home with God! Just as the body processes provide all of the means for a helpless cell to become a full-term baby, so God has provided every possible means through the Holy Spirit, the Word and the Church for His children to come to "full term" so that they may make a glorious transition into His presence! Like any compassionate Father, God will send chastisement, if necessary, to encourage obedience, but He would much rather *love* us into the kingdom!

In the world, it is sometimes the death of a loved one that becomes a catalyst to bring a family together or closer to God. The same is true of the family of God as manifested in the death of God's "only begotten" Son. His death, burial and resurrection as symbolized by the baptism of the believer becomes the common place of agreement for those "many brethren" who will follow Jesus Christ in obedience. The Cross, the picture of death, is the universal meeting ground for the body of Christ. It is the same death through which we—by faith —must all pass as we leave this world and are gloriously resurrected into the next:

> By a new and living way, which He hath consecrated for us, through the veil, that is to say, His flesh. (Hebrews 10:20)

> I am the resurrection and the life: he that believeth in Me, though he were dead, yet shall he live: and whosoever liveth and believeth in Me shall never die. Believest thou this? (John 11:25–26)

Conclusion

A Word from the Author

Perhaps you have read this book and are wondering how you can have assurance of salvation in your own life. This is an issue that can ultimately be settled only between you and God, but sometimes it is helpful to hear about another person's salvation experience or "testimony."

As a twelve-year-old boy growing up on a farm in North Dakota, I was, by any societal standard of reference, a *good* kid. However, while attending church services one Sunday morning I was suddenly overwhelmed with an awareness of the presence of sin in my life. Under conviction, I asked the pastor how I could be forgiven. I was greatly disturbed by the answer. He replied, *"I don't know."*

Although I could not be classified as a great sinner, *guilt* was very real and troubling to me and would continue to be an unresolved issue in my life for many years.

I began drinking when I was in college and this habit continued after I was accepted into veterinary school. I once visited a church and heard the pastor mention the fact that during God's judgments leading to the Exodus of Israel, the cattle belonging to the Egyptians were destroyed while those of Israel were spared. That same week one of my professors made reference to the possibility— given the differing conditions that existed between Goshen and the Nile floodplain—that *anthrax* was the disease that destroyed the Egyptian cattle. At that point, I concluded that everything could be explained in terms of scientific knowledge and I decided that I was an atheist.

At the age of twenty-one, I realized that I had become an alcoholic. With my medical training, I knew what alcohol was doing to my body and I resolved that I would stop drinking. I subsequently got through the withdrawal symptoms, but the craving for alcohol continued to torment me. In my *mind*, I was still an alcoholic.

During my final two years in veterinary school, I held several part-time jobs, including the care of animals that were being studied or treated on the school premises. One day, I arranged a Sunday afternoon date with a young lady and decided also that, to impress her, I would attend church that morning. Before preparing for church, I hurried off to clean up after a number of beagle puppies. I then proceeded to the dairy barn to attend to the sick bovines. As I prepared to leave, I was informed that my newest patient had arrived, a cow suffering from mastitis. After rushing to treat this condition, my first inclination was to either indicate "normal" or leave blank the place on the chart showing the animal's temperature. I knew that this would be dishonest, so I checked the cow only to find out that she had an extremely high fever resulting from another ailment that would have killed her if I had not administered intravenous antibiotics. Finally, I was again ready to leave but was informed that there were several calves also in need of treatment. By this time, I was thinking that I would either be late for church or miss it altogether.

I did manage to make it to church, although the service was already in progress. Any other motives I may have had for being in church that morning were quickly forgotten when, in a state of unprecedented introspection, I became aware that I did not like what I saw in *myself*. I didn't hear a word of the pastor's sermon because I was too busy examining what was in my own heart. I hated what I was doing, didn't love anyone and didn't think that anyone loved me.

Late that evening after my date, I returned to the campus to take care of the beagles. I was completely unprepared for what was about to happen. As I walked into the barn where the dogs were, I stopped in my tracks as the incredible, overpowering presence of *God* suddenly and supernaturally came over me and filled every corner of that building! There were no blinding lights, visions or other "special effects" and I heard no audible voices. But for the very first time, my spiritual eyes were opened, and this self-proclaimed atheist truly recognized that God was *real*. No vows, bargains or covenants were made on my part and I received no other great revelation, but I did realize that the unfathomable *love of God* had come down and occupied time and space long enough to speak *hope* into my life and to let me know that God was not only real, but He *cared*! God had chosen a lowly dog kennel as the venue for showing me that "I AM"! I had —at least as far as I was concerned—met Him face to face. I began openly praising God and the beagles were happily surprised when my cold, clinical approach inexplicably turned into affectionate and genuine caring. At that moment, I couldn't wait to tell someone about my *experience*. Later, whenever someone would inquire about my newly acquired religious zeal, I would tell them that I was now a "Christian."

I graduated from veterinary school and stayed on to do post-doctoral research and work on a graduate degree. Soon I met an attractive graduate chemistry student who—in a matter of weeks—would become my wife; she invited me to church, and I agreed to visit. The pastor preached from the scriptures for about an hour and then announced that it was time to stop. It was all I could do to restrain myself from jumping up from my seat and shouting, *"Don't stop!"*

Jan and I were married, and it was at this time that I sensed I had received a calling from God to preach the Gospel. We both dropped our plans for graduate degrees and moved to the Dallas–Fort Worth area. I attended seminary for a year, but it seemed that we were somehow outside of God's will, and I proceeded to open my own small animal hospital in Dallas. Before long, opportunities opened up for me to teach Sunday school and even preach in churches. However, my physical health had begun to deteriorate, and at under five feet, nine inches tall, my weight had dropped to 112 pounds! I was consuming a full box of antacid tablets a day just in order to be able to eat at all. I couldn't sleep at night because I was afraid I that would never wake up.

Finally, one day, I picked up a Bible and said, "God, You say in the scriptures that You will show us what we need… God, *do it*!" My insomnia provided a perfect excuse for reading the scriptures at night, and the following verses became particularly disturbing to me. I would read them over and over, and as I did so, I would find myself nearly overcome by chills and a profound sense of *fear*.

> Enter ye in at the [narrow] gate: for wide is the gate, and broad is the way, that leadeth to destruction, and many there be which go in threat: because [narrow] is the gate, and [narrow] is the way, which leadeth unto life, and few there be that find it. (Matthew 7:13–14)

> Not everyone that saith unto Me, "Lord, Lord," shall enter into the kingdom of Heaven; but he that doeth the will of My Father which is in Heaven. Many will say to Me in that day, "Lord, Lord, have we not prophesied in Thy name? And in Thy name have cast out devils? And in Thy name done many wonderful works?" And then will I profess unto them, "I never knew you: depart from Me, ye that work iniquity." (Matthew 7:21–23)

Many people had told me that my dramatic encounter with God in the barn at veterinary school had been a conversion experience similar to Paul's on the road to Damascus. I began to search out the scriptural account of Paul's conversion and came across the words of Ananias: "And now why tarriest thou?

Arise, and be baptized, and wash away thy sins, *calling on the name of the Lord*" (Acts 22:16). I suddenly recognized that I had not been born again in the barn while caring for the beagles. I had never called on the name of Jesus asking Him to take over control of my life!

On August 24, 1970, in our apartment with my wife by my side, I got on my knees and asked Jesus to forgive me and—in good Christian vernacular—to come into my life and be my *Lord* and *Savior*. My prayer was immediately answered and instantly guilt was *gone*. I knew that I was going to heaven and I could honestly say that I had *peace*. The residual craving for alcohol had disappeared; I was reminded of 2 Corinthians 5:17: "Therefore if any man be in Christ, he is a new creature: old things are passed away; behold, all things are become new" (2 Corinthians 5:17). I was no longer an alcoholic.

Perhaps you find yourself in a spiritual void and you recognize that there is no *peace* within you. In reality you have no capacity for giving or receiving God's *love*. You may be overwhelmed by a sense of fear, guilt, or remorse. You may be living in confusion and defeat and going through the motions of life without hope of ever finding the path to true joy and happiness. Perhaps you were even raised in the church. But you now recognize—regardless of what may have happened in the past—that you are *powerless* to change and the life of Christ is not resident within your own spirit. At this point, maybe you see yourself like that little unfertilized oocyte that is "alive" but desperately *incomplete*. You may recognize that you have been born of the *water*, but not of the *Spirit!*

God doesn't play games with your salvation. If you come to Him really wanting to know the truth, you will find it! People who have had a legitimate salvation experience and who have continued to walk with God *know* they are saved, even when they are struggling with sin and difficulty in their lives. If you genuinely believe in your heart that God raised Jesus from the dead, and you have been supernaturally drawn by the Holy Spirit to a place of complete honesty where you are willing to turn from your sins and surrender unconditional control of your life to Christ, there remains only one thing to be done: "*For whosoever shall call upon the name of the Lord shall be* saved" (Romans 10:13). Your prayer to God, out of your own heart and in your own words could be as simple as the childlike petition, "Help me!"

That if thou shalt confess with thy mouth the Lord Jesus, and shall believe in thine heart that God hath raised Him from the dead, Thou shalt be saved. For with the heart man believeth unto righteousness; and with the mouth confession is made unto salvation. (Romans 10:9–10)

Salvation is not about *feelings*, but when the Father, Son, and Holy Spirit come to reside in your own newly born spirit, you cannot help but feel *something*, even if it is only the very real sense that you have been *forgiven*. If you know with certainty that you have been born again by faith into God's family, simply thank Him and begin to associate with other believers who share your determination to walk with God. May God bless and keep you!

About the Author

The author grew up on a large ranch in North Dakota where his family had a dairy and raised both commercial and registered Herefords. They grew wheat, durum, barley, oats, and alfalfa hay. Growing up on a farm and ranch gave Ernest insight into the Scriptures as many illustrations in the Word of God are related to sheep, goats, and growing grain.

While in high school, Ernest studied a curriculum geared to be an engineer but changed to veterinary medicine at North Dakota State University. He received his DVM from Oklahoma State University. While doing postdoctoral research at OSU, he met his wife Jan, who was doing graduate work in chemistry. They were married eleven weeks later in 1966. After moving to Dallas, Texas, Ernest eventually had his own animal hospital. He received Jesus as his Savior on August 21, 1970, and soon started an outreach Bible study for hippies. This outreach became a church that Ernest pastored while still practicing veterinary medicine. After selling his veterinary practice at age sixty-two, he went to firefighter school and became a volunteer firefighter, and he is currently the chaplain of the Melissa Fire Department. Ernest and his wife Jan have four sons, five granddaughters, and one grandson.

www.ingramcontent.com/pod-product-compliance
Lightning Source LLC
Chambersburg PA
CBHW050729010526
44107CB00009B/794